The Marriage of Bette and Boo

The Marriage
of
Bette and Boo

by Christopher Durang

Nelson Doubleday, Inc.
Garden City, New York

To my mother

THE MARRIAGE OF BETTE AND BOO was first presented by the New York Shakespeare Festival (Joseph Papp, President) at the Public/Newman Theater in New York City on May 16, 1985. It was directed by Jerry Zaks; the scenery was by Loren Sherman; the costumes were by William Ivey Long; the lighting was by Paul Gallo; the original music was by Richard Peaslee; the hair was designed by Ron Frederick; the associate producer was Jason Steven Cohen; the production stage manager was James Harker; the stage manager was Pamela Singer. The cast was as follows:

BETTE BRENNAN	*Joan Allen*
MARGARET BRENNAN, her mother	*Patricia Falkenhain*
PAUL BRENNAN, her father	*Bill McCutcheon*
JOAN BRENNAN, her sister	*Mercedes Ruehl*
EMILY BRENNAN, her sister	*Kathryn Grody*
BOO HUDLOCKE	*Graham Beckel*
KARL HUDLOCKE, his father	*Bill Moor*
SOOT HUDLOCKE, his mother	*Olympia Dukakis*
FATHER DONNALLY/DOCTOR	*Richard B. Shull*
MATT	*Christopher Durang*

Understudies: Dalton Dearborn, Patrick Garner, Lizbeth MacKay, Rose Arrick, Ann Hilliary. During the final week, Mr. Dearborn and Ms. Hilliary played Karl and Soot.

THE MARRIAGE OF BETTE AND BOO has a long history. A fifty minute version was presented at the Yale School of Drama and at the Williamstown Theatre's Second Company. The Public Theatre production was the premiere of the expanded version.

The Marriage of Bette and Boo

CAST OF CHARACTERS

BETTE BRENNAN
MARGARET BRENNAN, her mother
PAUL BRENNAN, her father
JOAN BRENNAN, her sister
EMILY BRENNAN, her sister
BOO HUDLOCKE
KARL HUDLOCKE, his father
SOOT HUDLOCKE, his mother
FR. DONNALLY
DOCTOR
MATT

List of scenes:

Act II

ACT ONE

ACT I

Scene 1 *All the characters, in various wedding apparel, stand together to sing: the Brennan family, the Hudlocke family. Matthew stands apart from them.*

ALL: *(Sing)*
  God bless Bette and Boo and Skippy,
  Emily and Boo,
  Margaret, Matt, and Betsy Booey,
  Mommy, Tommy too,

  Betty Betsy Booey Boozey,
  Soot, Karl, Matt, and Paul,
  Margaret Booey, Joanie Phooey,
  God bless us one and all.
(The characters now call out to one another.)
BETTE: Booey? Booey? Skippy?
BOO: Pop?
MARGARET: Emily, dear?
BETTE: Booey?
BOO: Bette?
KARL: Is that Bore?
SOOT: Karl? Are you there?
JOAN: Nikkos!
BETTE: Skippy! Skippy!
EMILY: Are you all right, Mom?
BETTE: Booey, I'm calling you!
MARGARET: Paul? Where are you?
JOAN: Nikkos!
BOO: Bette? Betsy?
BETTE: Boo? Boo?
(Flash of light on the characters, as if their picture is being

...ken. Lights off the Brennans and Hudlockes. Light on Matt, late twenties or so. He speaks to the audience.)

MATT: If one looks hard enough, one can usually see the order that lies beneath the surface. Just as dreams must be put in order and perspective in order to understand them, so must the endless details of waking life be ordered and then carefully considered. Once these details have been considered, generalizations about them must be made. These generalizations should be written down legibly, and studied. *The Marriage of Bette and Boo.*

(Matt exits. Characters assume their places for photographs before the wedding. Boo stands to the side with his parents, Karl and Soot. Bette, in a wedding gown, poses for pictures with her family: Margaret, her mother; Emily, her sister, holding a cello; Joan, another sister, who is pregnant and is using nose spray; and Paul, her father. Bette, Margaret, Emily smile, looking out. Paul looks serious, fatherly. Joan looks sort of grouchy. Lights flash. They change positions.)

MARGARET: You look lovely, Bette.

EMILY: You do. Lovely.

MARGARET: A lovely bride. Smile for the camera, girls. *(Speaking out to either audience or to unseen photographer.)* Bette was always the most beautiful of my children. We used to say that Joanie was the most striking, but Bette was the one who looked beautiful all the time. And about Emily we used to say her health wasn't good.

EMILY: That's kind of you to worry, Mom, but I'm feeling much better. My asthma is hardly bothering me at all today. *(Coughs lightly.)*

MARGARET: Boo seems a lovely boy. Betsy, dear, why do they call him Boo?

BETTE: It's a nickname.

MARGARET: Don't you think Bette looks lovely, Joanie?

JOAN: *(Without enthusiasm.)* She does. You look lovely, Bette.

MARGARET: Where is Nikkos, dear?

JOAN: He's not feeling well. He's in the bathroom.

EMILY: Do you think we should ask Nikkos to play his saxophone with us, Joan dear?

JOAN: A saxophone would sound ridiculous with your cello, Emily.

EMILY: But Nikkos might feel left out.

JOAN: He'll probably stay in the bathroom anyway.

BETTE: Nikkos seems crazy. *(Joan glares at her.)* I wish you and Nikkos could've had a big wedding, Joanie.

MARGARET: Well, your father didn't much like Nikkos. It just didn't seem appropriate. *(Emily coughs softly.)* Are you all right, Emily?

EMILY: It's nothing, Mom.

JOAN: You're not going to get sick, are you?

EMILY: No. I'm sure I won't.

MARGARET: Emily, dear, please put away your cello. It's too large.

EMILY: I can't find the case.

(Joan uses her nose spray.)

BETTE: I can't wait to have a baby, Joanie.

JOAN: Oh yes?

MARGARET: *(Out to front again.)* Betsy was always the mother of the family, we'd say. She and her brother Tom. Played with dolls all day long, they did. Now Joanie hated dolls. If you gave Joanie a doll, she put it in the oven.

JOAN: I don't remember that, Mom.

BETTE: I love dolls.

EMILY: Best of luck, Bette. *(Kisses her; to Joan.)* Do you think Nikkos will be offended if we don't ask him to play with us?

JOAN: Emily, don't go on about it.

EMILY: Nikkos is a wonderful musician.

BETTE: So are you, Emily.

MARGARET: I just hope he's a good husband. Booey seems very nice, Betsy.

BETTE: I think I'll have a large family.

(Lights flash, taking a photo of the Brennans. Lights dim on them. Lights now pick up Boo, Karl, and Soot, who now pose for pictures.)

KARL: It's almost time, Bore.

BOO: Almost, Pop.

SOOT: Betsy's very pretty, Booey. Don't you think Betsy's pretty, Karl?

KARL: She's pretty. You're mighty old to be getting married, Bore. How old are you?

BOO: Thirty-two, Pop.

SOOT: That's not old, Karl.

KARL: Nearly over the hill, Bore.

SOOT: Don't call Booey "Bore" today, Karl. Someone might misunderstand.

KARL: Nobody will misunderstand.

(Photo flash. Enter Father Donnally. The families take their place on either side of him. Bette and Boo come together, and stand before him.)

FATHER DONNALLY: We are gathered here in the sight of God to join this man and this woman in the sacrament of holy matrimony. Do you, Bette . . . ?

BETTE: *(To Boo.)* I do.

FATHER DONNALLY: And do you, Boo . . . ?

BOO: *(To Bette.)* I do.

FATHER DONNALLY: *(Sort of to himself.)* Take this woman to be your lawfully wedded . . . I do, I do. *(Back to formal sounding.)* I pronounce you man and wife.

(Bette and Boo kiss. Karl throws a handful of rice at them, somewhat hostilely. This bothers no one.)

JOAN: Come on, Emily.

(Emily and Joan step forward. Paul gets Emily a chair to sit in when she plays her cello. He carries a flute.)

EMILY: And now, in honor of our dear Bette's wedding, I will play the cello and my father will play the flute, and my wonderful sister Joanie will sing the Schubert lied *Lachen und Weinen*, which translates as "Laughing and Crying." *(Joan gets in position to sing. Paul holds his flute to his mouth. Emily sits in her chair, puts the cello between her legs, and raises her bow. Long pause.)* I can't remember it.

JOAN: *(Very annoyed.)* It starts on A, Emily.

EMILY: *(Tries again; stops.)* I'm sorry. I'm sorry, Bette. I can't remember it.

(Everyone looks a little disappointed and disgruntled with Emily. Photo flash. Lights change. Spot on Matt.)

Scene 2   *Matt addresses the audience.*

MATT: When ordering reality, it is necessary to accumulate all the facts pertaining to the matter at hand. When all the facts are not immediately available, one must try to reconstruct them by considering oral history—hearsay, gossip, and apocryphal stories. And then with perseverance and intelligence, the analysis of these facts should bring about understanding. The honeymoon of Bette and Boo.

(Matt exits. Enter Bette, still in her wedding dress. In the fol-

lowing speech, and much of the time, Bette talks cheerfully and quickly, making no visible connections between her statements.)

BETTE: Hurry up, Boo. I want to use the shower. *(Speaks to audience, who seem to her a great friend.)* First I was a tomboy. I used to climb trees and beat up my brother Tom. Then I used to try to break my sister Joanie's voice box because she liked to sing. She always scratched me though, so instead I tried to play Emily's cello. Except I don't have a lot of musical talent, but I'm very popular. And I know more about the cello than people who don't know anything. I don't like the cello, it's too much work and besides, keeping my legs open that way made me feel funny. I asked Emily if it made her feel funny and she didn't know what I meant; and then when I told her she cried for two whole hours and then went to confession twice, just in case the priest didn't understand her the first time. Dopey Emily. She means well. *(Calls offstage.)* Booey! I'm pregnant! *(To audience.)* Actually I couldn't be, because I'm a virgin. A married man tried to have an affair with me, but he was married and so it would have been pointless. I didn't know he was married until two months ago. Then I met Booey, sort of on the rebound. He seems fine, though. *(Calls out.)* Booey! *(To audience.)* I went to confession about the cello practicing, but I don't think the priest heard me. He didn't say anything. He didn't even give me a penance. I wonder if nobody was in there. But as long as your conscience is all right, then so is your soul. *(Calls, giddy, happy.)* Booey, come on!

(Bette runs off. Lights change. Spot on Matt.)

Scene 3   *Matt addresses the audience.*

MATT: Margaret gives Emily advice.
(Matt exits. Enter Margaret, Emily, holding her cello.)
EMILY: Mom, I'm so upset that I forgot the piece at the wedding. Bette looked angry. When I write an apology, should I send it to Bette, or to Bette *and* Boo?
MARGARET: Emily, dear, don't go on about it.
(Lights change. Spot on Matt.)

Scene 4   *Matt addresses the audience.*

MATT: The honeymoon of Bette and Boo, continued.
*(Matt exits. Enter Bette and Boo, wrapped in a large sheet and
looking happy. They stand smiling for a moment. They should
still be in their wedding clothes—Bette minus her veil, Boo
minus his tie and jacket.)*
BETTE: That was better than a cello, Boo.
BOO: You're mighty good-looking, gorgeous.
BETTE: Do you think I'm prettier than Polly Lydstone?
BOO: Who?
BETTE: I guess you don't know her. I want to have lots of
children, Boo. Eight. Twelve. Did you read *Cheaper by the
Dozen?*
BOO: I have to call my father about a new insurance deal we're
handling. *(Takes phone from beneath the sheets; talks qui-
etly into it.)* Hello, Pop . . .
BETTE: *(To audience.)* Lots and lots of children. I loved the
movie *Skippy* with Jackie Cooper. I cried and cried. I always
loved little boys. Where is my pocketbook? Find it for me,
Boo.
*(The pocketbook is in full sight, but Bette doesn't seem to
notice it.)*
BOO: I'm talking to Pop, Bette. What is it, Pop?
BETTE: *(To audience.)* When I was a little girl, I used to love to
mind Jimmy Winkler. "Do you want me to watch Jimmy?"
I'd say to Mrs. Winkler. He was five years old and had short
stubby legs. I used to dress him up as a lamp shade and walk
him to town. I put tassels on his toes and taped doilies on his
knees, and he'd scream and scream. My mother said, "Betsy,
why are you crying about *Skippy*, it's only a movie, it's not
real." But I didn't believe her. Bonnie Wilson was my best
friend and she got tar all over her feet. Boo, where are you?
BOO: I'm here, angel. No, not you, Pop. No, I was talking to
Bette. Here, why don't you speak to her? *(Hands Bette the
phone.)* Here, Bette, it's Pop.
BETTE: Hello there, Mr. Hudlocke. How are you? And Mrs.
Hudlocke? I cried and cried at the movie *Skippy* because I
thought it was real. Bonnie Wilson and I were the two
stupidest in the class. Mrs. Sullivan used to say, "The two

stupidest in math are Bonnie and Betsy. Bonnie, your grade is eight, and Betsy, your grade is five." Hello? Hello? *(To Boo.)* We must have been cut off, Boo. Where is my pocketbook?

BOO: Here it is, beautiful.

(Boo gives her the pocketbook that has been in full sight all along.)

BETTE: I love you, Boo.

Scene 5　*Emily sits at her cello.*

EMILY: I can't remember it. *(She gets up and addresses her chair.)* It starts on A, Emily. *(She sits down, tries to play.)* I'm sorry. I'm sorry, Bette. I can't remember it.

(Enter Joan with scissors.)

JOAN: It may start on A, Emily. But it ends now.

(Joan raises scissors up. Freeze and/or lights change.)

Scene 6　*Matt addresses the audience.*

MATT: At the suggestion of *Redbook*, Bette refashions her wedding gown into a cocktail dress. Then she and Boo visit their in-laws. Bette is pregnant for the first time.

(Matt exits. Bette, Boo, Karl, Soot. Bette is in a shortened, simplified version of her wedding dress.)

SOOT: How nice that you're going to have a baby.

KARL: Have another drink, Bore.

BETTE: *(To Soot.)* I think Booey drinks too much. Does Mr. Hudlocke drink too much?

SOOT: I never think about it.

KARL: Soot, get me and Bore another drink.

(Boo and Karl are looking over papers, presumably insurance.)

BETTE: Don't have another one, Boo.

SOOT: *(Smiles, whispers.)* I think Karl drinks too much, but when he's sober he's really very nice.

BETTE: I don't think Boo should drink if I'm going to have a baby.

SOOT: If it's a boy, you can name him Boo, and if it's a girl you can call her Soot after me.

BETTE: How did you get the name "Soot"?

SOOT: Oh, you know. The old saying "She fell down the chimney and got covered with soot."

BETTE: What saying?

SOOT: Something about that. Karl might remember. Karl, how did I get the name "Soot"?

KARL: Get the drinks, Soot.

SOOT: All right.

KARL: *(To Bette.)* Soot is the dumbest white woman alive.

SOOT: Oh, Karl. *(Laughs, exits.)*

BETTE: I don't want you to get drunk again, Boo. Joanie's husband Nikkos may lock himself in the bathroom, but he doesn't drink.

BOO: Bette, Pop and I are looking over these papers.

BETTE: I'm your wife.

BOO: Bette, you're making a scene.

KARL: Your baby's going to be all mouth if you keep talking so much. You want to give birth to a mouth, Bette?

BETTE: All right. I'm leaving.

BOO: Bette. Can't you take a joke?

BETTE: It's not funny.

KARL: I can tell another one. There was this drunken airline stewardess who got caught in the propeller . . .

BETTE: I'm leaving now, Boo. *(Exits.)*

BOO: Bette. I better go after her. *(Starts to exit.)*

KARL: Where are you going, Bore?

BOO: Bette's a little upset, Pop. I'll see you later.

(Boo exits. Enter Soot with drinks.)

SOOT: Where's Booey, Karl?

KARL: He isn't here.

SOOT: I know. Where did he go?

KARL: Out the door.

SOOT: Did you say something to Bette, Karl?

KARL: Let's have the drinks, Soot.

SOOT: You know, I really can't remember how everyone started calling me Soot. Can you, Karl?

KARL: Go into your dance, Soot.

SOOT: Oh, Karl. *(Laughs.)*

KARL: Go get the veils and start in. The shades are down.

SOOT: Karl, I don't know what you're talking about.

KARL: You're the dumbest white woman alive. I rest my case.

(Soot laughs. Lights change.)

Scene 7 *Matt addresses the audience.*

MATT: Bette goes to Margaret, her mother, for advice.
(Matt exits. Bette, Margaret. Emily on the floor, writing a note. Paul, the father, is also present.)
BETTE: Mom, Boo drinks. And his father insulted me.
MARGARET: Betsy, dear, marriage is no bed of roses.
EMILY: Mom, is the phrase "my own stupidity" hyphenated?
MARGARET: No, Emily. She's apologizing to Joanie again about forgetting the piece at the wedding. Joanie *was* very embarrassed.
BETTE: How can I make Boo stop drinking?
MARGARET: I'm sure it's not a serious problem, Betsy.
BETTE: Poppa, what should I do?
PAUL: W##hh, ah%#% enntgh oo sh#$w auns$$dr ehvg### ing%%#s ahm.
(NOTE TO READER AND/OR ACTOR: *Paul is meant to be the victim of a stroke. His mind is still functioning well, but his ability to speak is greatly impaired. Along these lines, I give him specific lines to say and be motivated by, but the audience and the other characters in the play should genuinely be unable to make out almost anything that he says—though they can certainly follow any emotional colorings he gives. I have found it useful for actors who read the part of Paul to say the lines written in the brackets, but to drop almost all of the consonants and to make the tongue go slack, so that poor Paul's speech is almost all vowels, mixed in with an occasional, inexplicable group of consonants. Paul's first line up above— emphasizing that no one should be able to make out almost any of it—would be: "Well, I think you should consider giving things time."*)
BETTE: *What* should I do?
PAUL: *(Angry that he can't be understood.)* On####%t ump oo%#% onoosns#$s. Eggh ing ahm#$. [Don't jump to conclusions. Give things time.]
MARGARET: Paul, I've asked you not to speak. We can't understand you.
EMILY: Mom, how do you spell "mea culpa"?
MARGARET: Emily, Latin is pretentious in an informal letter. Joanie will think you're silly.

EMILY: This one is to Father Donnally.

MARGARET: M-E-A C-U-L-P-A.

BETTE: Boo's father has given him a very bad example. *(Enter Joan, carrying a piece of paper.)* Oh, Joan, quick—do you think when I have my baby, it will make Boo stop . . .

JOAN: Wait a minute. *(To Emily.)* Emily, I got your note. Now listen to me closely. *(With vehemence.)* I *forgive* you, I *forgive* you, I *forgive* you.

EMILY: *(A bit startled.)* Oh. Thank you.

JOAN: *(To Bette.)* Now, what did you want?

BETTE: Do you think when I have my baby, it will make Boo stop drinking and bring him and me closer together?

JOAN: I have no idea.

BETTE: Well, but hasn't your having little Mary Frances made things better between you and Nikkos? He isn't still disappearing for days, is he?

JOAN: Are you trying to make me feel bad about my marriage?

EMILY: I'm sorry, Joanie.

JOAN: What?

EMILY: If I made you feel bad about your marriage.

JOAN: Oh, shut up. *(Exits.)*

BETTE: *(To Margaret.)* She's so nasty. Did you punish her enough when she was little?

MARGARET: She's just tired because little Mary Frances cries all the time. She really is a dreadful child.

BETTE: I love babies. Poppa, don't you think my baby will bring Boo and me closer together?

PAUL: Aszzs&* ot uh er#ry owowd# @ eeah oo ah uh ayee, ehtte. [That's not a very good reason to have a baby, Bette.]

(Bette looks at Paul blankly. Lights change.)

Scene 8 *Matt addresses the audience.*

MATT: Twenty years later, Boo has dinner with his son.

(Boo and Matt sit at a table.)

BOO: Well, how are things up at Dartmouth, Skip? People in the office ask me how my Ivy League son is doing.

MATT: It's all right.

BOO: Are there any pretty girls up there?

MATT: Uh huh.

BOO: So what are you learning up there?

1

MATT: Tess of the d'Urbervilles is a masochist.

BOO: What?

MATT: It's a novel we're reading. *(Mumbles.) Tess of the d'Urbervilles.*

BOO: *(Laughs.)* A man needs a woman, son. I miss your mother. I'd go back with her in a minute if she wanted. She's not in love with her family anymore, and I think she knows that drinking wasn't that much of a problem. I think your old man's going to get teary for a second. I'm just an old softie. *(Boo blinks his eyes, wipes them. Matt exits, embarrassed. Boo doesn't notice but addresses the chair as if Matt were still there.)* I miss your mother, Skip. Nobody should be alone. Do you have any problems, son, you want to talk over? Your old man could help you out.

(Boo waits for an answer. Lights change.)

Scene 9 *Matt addresses the audience.*

MATT: The first child of Bette and Boo.

(Matt exits. Enter Boo, Karl, Soot, Margaret, Emily with her cello, Joan, Paul. They all stand in a line and wait expectantly. Enter the doctor, who is played by the same actor who plays Father Donnally.)

DOCTOR: She's doing well. Just a few more minutes. *(Exits.)*

EMILY: Oh God, make her pain small. Give me the pain rather than her. *(Winces in pain.)*

MARGARET: Emily, behave, this is a hospital.

BOO: Pop, I hope it's a son.

KARL: This calls for a drink. Soot, get Bore and me a drink.

SOOT: Where would I go?

KARL: A drink, Soot.

SOOT: Karl, you're teasing me again.

KARL: All right, I won't talk to you.

SOOT: Oh, please. Please talk to me. Booey, talk to your father.

BOO: Come on, Pop. We'll have a drink afterwards.

SOOT: Karl, I'll get you a drink. *(To Margaret.)* Where would I go? *(To Karl.)* Karl?

KARL: This doctor know what he's doing, Bore?

SOOT: Karl? Wouldn't you like a drink?

EMILY: It's almost here. *(Having an experience of some sort.)* Oh no, no, no no no no.

MARGARET: Emily!

KARL: This Betsy's sister, Bore?

BOO: Pop, I hope it's a boy.

KARL: You were a boy, Bore. *(Enter the doctor, holding the baby in a blue blanket.)* This is it, Bore.

EMILY: In the name of the Father, and of the Son, and of the Holy Ghost.

DOCTOR: It's dead. The baby's dead. *(He drops it on the floor.)*

EMILY: *(Near collapse.)* Oh no!

JOAN: I win the bet.

MARGARET: I'm here, Betsy, it's all right. *(Paul picks up the baby.)* Paul, put the baby down. That's disrespectful.

PAUL: Buh uh ayee ah#$# ehh#! [But the baby's not dead.]

MARGARET: Don't shout. I can understand you.

PAUL: *(To doctor.)* Uh ayee ah#$# ehh#! Yrr uh ahherr, ann## oo ee, uh ayee ah#$# ehh#! [The baby's not dead. You're a doctor, can't you see, the baby's not dead.]

DOCTOR: *(Takes the baby.)* Oh, you're right. It's not dead. Mr. Hudlocke, you have a son.

KARL: Congratulations, Bore.

EMILY: Thank you, God. *(Enter Bette, radiant. She takes the baby.)*

BETTE: *(To audience.)* We'll call the baby Skippy.

EMILY: It has to be a saint's name, Bette.

BETTE: Mind your business, Emily.

MARGARET: Betsy, dear, Emily's right. Catholics have to be named after saints. Otherwise they can't be baptized.

BOO: Boo.

MARGARET: There is no Saint Boo.

EMILY: We should call it Margaret in honor of Mom.

BETTE: It's a boy.

EMILY: We should call him Paul in honor of Dad.

MARGARET: Too common.

SOOT: I always liked Clarence.

JOAN: I vote for Boo.

MARGARET: *(Telling her to behave.)* Joanie.

KARL: Why not name it after a household appliance?

SOOT: Karl. *(Laughs.)*

KARL: Egg beater. Waffle iron. Bath mat.

BETTE: *(To audience.)* Matt. I remember a little boy named Matt who looked just like a wind-up toy. We'll call him Matt.

BOO: It's a boy, Pop.

EMILY: Is Matt a saint's name, Bette?

BETTE: Matt*hew*, Emily. Maybe if you'd finally join the convent, you'd learn the apostles' names.

EMILY: Do you think I should join a convent?

BETTE: *(To audience.)* But his nickname's going to be Skippy. My very favorite movie.

(Lights change.)

Scene 10 *Matt addresses the audience.*

MATT: *My Very Favorite Movie,* an essay by Matthew Hudlocke. My very favorite movie . . . are . . . *Nights of Cabiria, 8½, Citizen Kane, L'Avventura, The Seventh Seal, Persona, The Parent Trap, The Song of Bernadette, Potemkin, The Fire Within, The Bells of St. Mary's, The Singing Nun, The Dancing Nun, The Nun on the Fire Escape Outside My Window, The Nun That Caused the Chicago Fire, The Nun Also Rises, The Nun Who Came to Dinner, The Caucasian Chalk Nun, Long Day's Journey into Nun, None But the Lonely Heart,* and *The Nun Who Shot Liberty Valance.*

Page two. In the novels of Thomas Hardy, we find a deep and unrelieved pessimism. Hardy's novels, set in his home town of Wessex, contrast nature outside of man with the human nature inside of man, coming together inexorably to cause human catastrophe. The sadness in Hardy—his lack of belief that a benevolent God watches over human destiny, his sense of the waste and frustration of the average human life, his forceful irony in the face of moral and metaphysical questions—is part of the late Victorian mood. We can see something like it in A. E. Housman, or in Emily's life. Shortly after Skippy's birth, Emily enters a convent, but then leaves the convent due to nerves. Bette becomes pregnant for the second time. Boo continues to drink. If psychiatrists had existed in nineteenth century Wessex, Hardy might suggest Bette and Boo seek counseling. Instead he has no advice to give them, and in 1886 he writes *The Mayor of Casterbridge.* This novel is one of Hardy's greatest successes, and Skippy studies it in college. When he is little, he studies *The Wind in the Willows* with Emily. And when he is very little, he studies drawing with Emily.

(Emily, Matt. Emily has brightly colored construction paper and crayons.)

EMILY: Hello, Skippy, dear. I thought we could do some nice arts and crafts today. Do you want to draw a cat or a dog?

MATT: A dog.

EMILY: All right, then I'll do a cat. *(They begin to draw.)* Here's the head, and here's the whiskers. Oh dear, it looks more like a clock. Oh, Skippy, yours is very good. I can tell it's a dog. Those are the ears, and that's the tail, right?

MATT: Yes.

EMILY: That's very good. And you draw much better than Mary Frances. I tried to interest her in drawing Babar the elephant the other day, but she doesn't like arts and crafts, and she scribbled all over the paper, and then she had a crying fit. *(Sits back.)* Oh dear. I shouldn't say she doesn't draw well, it sounds like a criticism of Joanie.

MATT: I won't tell.

EMILY: Yes, but it would be on my conscience. I better write Joanie a note apologizing. And really, Mary Frances draws *very* well, I didn't mean it when I said she didn't. She probably had a headache. I think I'll use this nice pink piece of construction paper to apologize to Joanie, and I'll apologize about forgetting the piece at your mother's wedding too. I've never been sure Joanie's forgiven me, even though she says she has. I don't know what else I can do except apologize. I don't have any money.

MATT: Your cat looks very good. It doesn't look like a clock.

EMILY: You're such a comfort, Skippy. I'll be right back. Why don't you pretend your dog is real, and you can teach it tricks while I'm gone.

(Emily exits. Matt makes "roll over" gesture to drawing, waits for response. Lights change. Matt exits.)

Scene 11   *Bette enters, carrying a chair. She sits on the chair.*

BETTE: *(To audience and/or herself.)* I'm going to pretend that I'm sitting in this chair. Then I'm going to pretend that I'm going to have another baby. And then I'm going to have another, and another and another. I'm going to pretend to have a big family. There'll be Skippy. And then all the A. A. Milne characters. Boo should join AA. There'll be Eeyore

and Pooh Bear and Christopher Robin and Tigger . . . My
family is going to be like an enormous orphanage. I'll be
their mother. Kanga and six hundred Baby Roos. Baby Roo is
Kanga's baby, but she's a mother to them all. Roo and Tigger
and Pooh and Christopher Robin and Eeyore and Owl, owl,
ow, ow, ow, ow, ow, ow, ow, ow! I'm giving birth, Mom. Roo
and Tigger and Boo and Pooh and Soot and Eeyore and Karl
and Betsy and Owl . . .

*(Enter quickly: Boo, Karl, Soot, Margaret, Paul, Emily, Joan.
They stand in their same hospital positions. Enter the doctor
with the baby in a blue blanket.)*

DOCTOR: The baby's dead. *(Drops it on the floor.)*

MARGARET: Nonsense. That's what he said about the last one,
didn't he, Paul?

DOCTOR: This time it's true. It *is* dead.

BETTE: Why?

DOCTOR: The reason the baby is dead is this: Mr. Hudlocke has
Rh positive blood.

KARL: Good for you, Bore!

DOCTOR: Mrs. Hudlocke has Rh negative blood.

BETTE: Like Kanga.

DOCTOR: And so the mother's Rh negative blood fights the
baby's Rh positive blood and so: the mother kills the baby.

EMILY: *(Rather horrified.)* Who did this??? The mother did
this???

KARL: You married a winner, Bore.

BOO: The baby came. And it was dead. *(Picks up baby.)*

SOOT: Poor Booey.

BETTE: But I'll have other babies.

DOCTOR: The danger for your health if you do and the likelihood of stillbirth are overwhelming considerations.

BOO: The baby came. And it was dead.

BETTE: Mama, tell him to go away.

MARGARET: There, there. Say something to her, Paul.

(Paul says nothing. Lights change.)

Scene 12   *Matt addresses the audience.*

MATT: Bette and Margaret visit Emily, who is in a rest home
due to nerves.

(Matt exits. Emily with her cello. Bette, Margaret. Bette seems very depressed, and keeps looking at the floor or looking off.)

EMILY: Oh, Mom, Bette. It's so good to see you. How are you feeling, Bette, after your tragedy?

MARGARET: Emily, don't talk about it. Change the subject.

EMILY: *(Trying desperately to oblige.)* Um . . . um . . . uh . . .

MARGARET: *(Looking around slightly.)* This is a very nice room for an institution. Bette, look up. Do you like the doctors, Emily?

EMILY: Yes, they're very good to me.

MARGARET: They should be. They're very expensive. I was going to ask your brother Tom for some money for your stay here, but he's really not . . . Oh, I didn't mean to mention Tom. Forget I said anything.

EMILY: Oh, what is it? Is he all right?

MARGARET: I shouldn't have mentioned it. Forget it, Emily.

EMILY: But what's the matter with him? Is he ill? Oh, Mom . . .

MARGARET: Now, Emily, don't go on about it. That's a fault of yours. If you had stayed in the convent, maybe you could have corrected that fault. Oh, I'm sorry. I didn't mean to bring up the convent.

EMILY: That's all right, Mom. *(Silence.)*

MARGARET: Besides, whatever happens, happens. Don't look that way, Emily. Change the subject.

EMILY: Um . . . uh . . .

MARGARET: There are many pleasant things in the world, think of them.

EMILY: *(Trying hard to think of something; then:)* How is Skippy, Bette?

BETTE: Who?

EMILY: Skippy.

BETTE: *(To Margaret.)* Who?

MARGARET: She means Baby Roo, dear.

BETTE: Oh, Roo. Yes. *(Stares off in distance blankly.)*

EMILY: Is he well?

MARGARET: *(Telling Emily to stop.)* He's fine, dear. Looks just like his mother.

EMILY: He's a lovely child. I look forward to seeing him when I finally leave here and get to go . . . *(Gets teary.)*

MARGARET: Emily, the doctors told me they're sure you're not here for life. Isn't that right, Bette? *(Whispers to Emily.)* The doctors say Bette shouldn't have any more babies.

EMILY: Oh dear. And Bette's a wonderful mother. Bette, dear, don't feel bad, you have the one wonderful child, and maybe someday God will make a miracle so you can have more children.

BETTE: *(The first sentence she's heard.)* I can have more children?

EMILY: Well, maybe God will make a *miracle* so you can.

BETTE: I can have a miracle?

EMILY: Well, you pray and ask for one.

MARGARET: Emily, miracles are very fine . . .

EMILY: Oh, I didn't think, I shouldn't have . . .

MARGARET: But now you've raised Betsy's hopes . . .

EMILY: Oh, Bette, listen to Mom . . . I'm so sorry . . .

BETTE: I CAN HAVE MORE CHILDREN!

MARGARET: That's right, Betsy. Emily, I know you didn't mean to bring this up . . .

EMILY: I'm so stupid . . .

MARGARET: But first you start in on your brother Tom who has a spastic colon and is drinking too much . . .

EMILY: Oh no!

BETTE: *(Very excited; overlapping with Margaret.)* I CAN HAVE MORE CHILDREN, I CAN HAVE MORE CHILDREN, I CAN HAVE MORE CHILDREN . . . *(etc.)*

MARGARET: *(Overlapping with Bette.)* . . . and has been fired and there's some crazy talk about him and some boy in high school, which I'm sure isn't true, and even if it is . . .

EMILY: Tom's all right, isn't he, it isn't true . . .

BETTE: . . . I CAN HAVE MORE CHILDREN! . . . *(etc.)*

MARGARET: I didn't mean to tell you, Emily, but you talk and talk . . .

BETTE: . . . I CAN HAVE MORE CHILDREN, I CAN HAVE MORE CHILDREN . . .

EMILY: Oh, Mom, I'm so sorry, I . . .

MARGARET: . . . and *talk* about a thing until you think your head is going to explode . . .

EMILY: *(Overlapping still.)* I'm so sorry, I . . . WAIT! *(Silence. Emily sits at her cello with great concentration, picks up the bow.)* I think I remember it. *(Listens, tries to remember the piece from the wedding, keeps trying out different opening notes. Margaret looks between the two girls.)*

MARGARET: I wish you two could see yourselves. *(Laughs merrily.)* You're both acting very funny. *(Laughs again.)* Come on, Betsy.
(Margaret and Bette exit, cheerful. Emily keeps trying to remember. Lights change.)

Scene 13 *Matt addresses the audience.*

MATT: Bette seeks definition of the word "miracle" from Father Donnally.
(Matt exits. Bette, Father Donnally. She kneels to him in the confessional, blesses herself.)
FATHER DONNALLY: Hello, Bette, how are you?
BETTE: I'm feeling much better after my tragedy.
FATHER DONNALLY: It's a cross to bear.
BETTE: Have you ever read *Winnie the Pooh*, Father? Most people think it's for children, but I never read it until I was an adult. The humor is very sophisticated.
FATHER DONNALLY: I'll have to read it sometime.
BETTE: Do you believe in miracles, Father?
FATHER DONNALLY: Miracles rarely happen, Bette.
BETTE: I do too! Thank you, Father. You've helped me make a decision.
(Lights change.)

Scene 14 *Matt addresses the audience.*

MATT: Soot gives Bette some advice.
(Matt exits. Bette, pregnant, Boo, Soot, Karl.)
BETTE: And then Father Donnally said that I should just keep trying and that even if this baby died, there would be at least one more baby that would live, and then I would be a mother as God meant me to be. Do you agree, Soot?
SOOT: I've never met this Father Donnally. Karl, Pauline has a retarded daughter, doesn't she? LaLa is retarded, isn't she? I mean, she isn't just slow, is she?
BETTE: I don't care if the child's retarded. Then that's God's will. I love retarded children. I like children more than I like people. Boo, you're drinking too much, it's not fair to me. If this baby dies, it's going to be your fault.

BOO: I don't think Father Donnally should have encouraged you about this. That's what I think.

BETTE: He's a priest. *(To Soot.)* Did you ever see Jackie Cooper as a child? I thought he was much cuter than Shirley Temple, what do you think, Soot?

KARL: Bore, my wife Soot hasn't said one sensible thing in thirty years of marriage . . .

SOOT: Oh, Karl . . . *(Laughs, flattered.)*

KARL: But your little wife has just said more senseless things in one ten-minute period than Soot here has said in thirty years of bondage.

SOOT: Oh, Karl. I never was one for talking.

BETTE: *(To Karl.)* Look here, you. I'm not afraid of you. I'm not going to let Boo push me to a breakdown the way you've pushed Soot. I'm stronger than that.

SOOT: Oh my. *(Laughs.)* Sit down, dear.

KARL: Tell the baby-maker to turn it down, Bore.

BOO: Bette, sit down.

BETTE: I want a marriage and a family and a home, and I'm going to have them, and if you won't help me, Boo, I'll have them without you. *(Exits.)*

KARL: Well, Bore, I don't know about you and your wife. Whatever one can say against your mother, and it's most everything *(Soot laughs)*, at least she didn't go around dropping dead children at every step of the way like some goddamned giddy farm animal.

SOOT: Karl, you shouldn't tease everyone so.

KARL: I don't like the way you're behaving today, Soot. *(Exits.)*

SOOT: *(Looks back to where Bette was.)* Bette, dear, let me give you some advice. Oh, that's right. She left. *(A moment of disorientation; looks at Boo.)* Boo, Karl's a lovely man most of the time, and I've had a very happy life with him, but I hope you'll be a little kinder than he was. Just a little. Anything is an improvement. I wish I had dead children. I wish I had two hundred dead children. I'd stuff them down Karl's throat. *(Laughs.)* Of course, I'm only kidding. *(Laughs some more. Lights change.)*

Scene 15 *Matt addresses the audience.*

MATT: Now the Mayor of Casterbridge, when drunk, sells his wife and child to someone he meets in a bar. Now Boo is considerably better behaved than this. Now the fact of the matter is that Boo isn't really an alcoholic at all, but drinks simply because Bette is such a terrible, unending nag. Or perhaps Boo *is* an alcoholic, and Bette is a terrible, unending nag in *reaction* to his drinking so much, and also because he just isn't "there" for her, any more than Clym Yeobright is really there for Eustacia Vye in *The Return of the Native*, although admittedly Eustacia Vye is very neurotic, but then so is Bette also.

　　Or perhaps it's the fault of the past history of stillbirths and the pressures that that history puts on their physical relationship. Perhaps blame can be assigned totally to the Catholic Church. Certainly Emily's guilt about leaving the convent and about everything else in the world can be blamed largely on the Catholic Church. *(Pleased.)* James Joyce can be blamed on the Catholic Church; but not really Thomas Hardy. And then in 1896 Hardy writes *Jude the Obscure*. And when Skippy is nine, Bette goes to the hospital for the third time. The third child of Bette and Boo.
(Matt exits. Lights change.)

Scene 16 *Everyone assembles, except for Bette: Boo, Karl, Soot, Margaret, Paul, Joan, Emily. They wait. Enter the doctor. He drops the baby on the floor, exits. Pause. Lights change.*

Scene 17 *Bette on the telephone, late at night.*

BETTE: Hello, Bonnie? This is Betsy. Betsy. *(To remind her.)* "Bonnie, your grade is eight, and Betsy, your grade is five." Yes, it's me. How are you? Oh, I'm sorry, I woke you? Well, what time is it? Oh, I'm sorry. But isn't Florida in a different time zone than we are? Oh. I thought it was. Oh well.
　　Bonnie, are you married? How many children do you have? Two. That's nice. Are you going to have any more?

Oh, I think you should. Yes, I'm married. To Boo. I wrote you. Oh, I never wrote you? How many years since we've spoken? Since we were fifteen. Well, I'm not a very good correspondent. Oh dear, you're yawning, I guess it's too late to have called. Bonnie, do you remember the beach and little Jimmy Winkler? I used to dress him up as a lamp shade, it was so cute. Oh. Well, do you remember when Miss Willis had me stand in the corner, and you stand in the wastebasket, and then your grandmother came to class that day? I thought you'd remember that. Oh, you want to go back to sleep?

Oh, I'm sorry. Bonnie, before you hang up, I've lost two babies. No, I don't mean misplaced, stupid, they died. I go through the whole nine-month period of carrying them, and then when it's over, they just take them away. I don't even see the bodies. Hello? Oh, I thought you weren't there. I'm sorry, I didn't realize it was so late. I thought Florida was Central Time or something. Yes, I got twelve in geography or something, you remember? "Betsy, your grade is twelve and Bonnie, your grade is . . ." What did you get in geography? Well, it's not important anyway. What? No, Boo's not home. Well, sometimes he just goes to a bar and then he doesn't come home until the bar closes, and some of them don't close at all and so he gets confused what time it is. Does your husband drink? Oh, that's good. What's his name? Scooter? Like bicycle? I like the name Scooter. I love cute things. Do you remember Jackie Cooper in *Skippy* and his best friend Sukey? I cried and cried. Hello, are you still there? I'm sorry, I guess I better let you go back to sleep. Good-bye, Bonnie, it was good to hear your voice. *(Hangs up. Lights change.)*

Scene 18 *Matt addresses the audience.*

MATT: Several months later, Bette and Boo have the two families over to celebrate Thanksgiving.
(Bette, Matt. Bette is on the warpath.)
BETTE: *(Calling off, nasty.)* Come *up* from the cellar, Boo. I'm not going to say it again. They're going to be here. *(To Matt.)* He's hidden a bottle behind the furnace.
MATT: Please stop shouting.

BETTE: Did you smell something on his breath?

MATT: I don't know. I didn't get that close.

BETTE: Can't you go up and kiss him?

MATT: I can't go up and kiss him for no reason.

BETTE: You're so unaffectionate. There's nothing wrong with a ten-year-old boy kissing his father.

MATT: I don't want to kiss him.

BETTE: Well, I think I smelled something. *(Enter Boo.)*

BOO: What are you talking about?

BETTE: You're always picking on me. I wasn't talking about anything. Set the table, Skippy. *(Matt exits.)*

BOO: When are they all coming?

BETTE: When do you think they're coming? Let me smell your breath.

BOO: Leave my breath alone.

BETTE: You've been drinking. You've got a funny look in your eye.

(Enter Matt, holding some silverware.)

MATT: Something's burning in the oven.

BETTE: Why can't you stop drinking? You don't care enough about me and Skippy to stop drinking, do you?

MATT: It's going to burn.

BETTE: You don't give me anything to be grateful for. You're just like your father. You're a terrible example to Skippy. He's going to grow up neurotic because of you.

MATT: I'll turn the oven off. *(Exits.)*

BOO: Why don't you go live with your mother, you're both so perfect.

BETTE: Don't criticize my mother.

(Enter Joan and Emily. Joan has a serving dish with candied sweet potatoes; Emily has a large gravy boat dish.)

EMILY: Happy Thanksgiving, Bette.

BETTE: Hush, Emily. You're weak, Boo. It's probably just as well the other babies have died.

EMILY: I brought the gravy.

BETTE: We don't care about the gravy, Emily. I want you to see a priest, Boo.

BOO: Stop talking. I want you to stop talking.

(Enter Margaret and Paul. Paul is holding a large cake.)

MARGARET: Hello, Betsy, dear.

BETTE: He's been drinking.

MARGARET: Let's not talk about it. Hello, Boo, Happy Thanks-giving.

BOO: Hello.

(Enter Soot and Karl. Soot is carrying a candelabra.)

SOOT: Hello, Margaret.

MARGARET: How nice to see you. Paul, you remember Mrs. Hudlocke?

PAUL: Icse oo ee oo, issizzse uhoch##. Iht oo ab uhulll ineing uh arreeng ace####? [Nice to see you, Mrs. Hudlocke. Did you have trouble finding a parking place?]

SOOT: I guess so. *(To everybody.)* I brought a candelabra.

BETTE: *(To Soot.)* You're his mother, I want you to smell his breath.

BOO: SHUT UP ABOUT MY BREATH!

(Boo accidentally knocks into Emily, who drops the gravy on the floor.)

BETTE: You've spilled the gravy all over the rug!

EMILY: I'm sorry.

BETTE: Boo did it!

BOO: I'll clean it up, I'll clean it up. *(Exits.)*

BETTE: I think he's hidden a bottle in the cellar.

EMILY: Joanie didn't drop the sweet potatoes.

SOOT: Are we early? *(Laughs.)*

KARL: Pipe down, Soot.

(Boo enters with a vacuum cleaner. All watch him as he starts to vacuum up the gravy.)

BETTE: What are you doing? Boo!

BOO: I can do it!

BETTE: You don't vacuum gravy!

BOO: I can do it!

BETTE: Stop it! You're ruining the vacuum!

SOOT: Oh dear. Let's go. *(Laughs.)* Good-bye, Booey.

(Karl and Soot exit.)

JOAN: I knew we shouldn't have had it here.

MARGARET: Come on, Betsy. Why don't you and Skippy stay with us tonight?

BETTE: YOU DON'T VACUUM GRAVY!

MARGARET: Let it alone, Betsy.

BETTE: You don't vacuum gravy. You don't vacuum gravy. You don't vacuum gravy!

BOO: *(Hysterical.)* WHAT DO YOU DO WITH IT THEN? TELL ME! WHAT DO YOU DO WITH IT?

BETTE: *(Quieter, but very upset.)* You get warm water, and a sponge, and you sponge it up.

(Bette and Boo stare at one another, spent.)

EMILY: Should we put the sweet potatoes in the oven?

(Matt exits.)

JOAN: Come on, Emily. Let's go home.

MARGARET: Betsy, if you and Skippy want to stay at our house tonight, just come over. Good-bye, Boo.

EMILY: *(Calls.)* Good-bye, Skippy.

(Margaret, Joan, Emily, and Paul exit. Enter Matt with a pan of water and two sponges. He hands them to Bette. Bette and Boo methodically sponge up the gravy. Music to the "Bette and Boo" theme in the background.)

BOO: *(Quietly.)* Okay, we'll soak it up with the sponge. That's what we're doing. We're soaking it up. *(They more or less finish with it.)* I'm going to take a nap.

(Boo lies down where he is, and falls asleep.)

BETTE: Boo? Boo? Booey? Boo?

(Enter Soot.)

SOOT: Did I lose an earring in here? Oh dear. He's just asleep, isn't he?

BETTE: Boo? Boo.

SOOT: He must have gotten tired. *(Holds up earring, to Matt.)* If you should see it, it looks just like this one. *(Laughs.)* Booey? *(Laughs.)* I think he's asleep. Good-bye, Booey. *(Exits.)*

BETTE: Boo? Booey?

MATT: Please don't try to wake him up. You'll just argue.

BETTE: All right. I won't try to wake him. *(Pause.)* Boo. Booey. *(She pushes his shoulder slightly.)* Boo. *(To Matt.)* I just want to get through to him about the gravy. *(To Boo.)* Boo. You don't vacuum gravy. Are you awake, Boo? Boo? I wonder if he's going to sleep through the night. I can wait. Boo. Booey.

(Bette looks at Matt, then back at Boo. Matt looks at both of them, then out to audience, exhausted and trapped, but with little actual expression on his face. Lights dim. End Act I.)

ACT TWO

ACT II

Scene 19 *Bette, Boo, Father Donnally down center. Matt to the side. All the others stand together as they did in the beginning to sing the "Bette and Boo" theme. Music introduction to the theme is heard.*

ALL: *(Except Bette, Boo, Father Donnally, Matt sing:)*
   Ninety-nine bottles of beer on the wall,
   Ninety-nine bottles of beer,
   Take one down, pass it around,
   Ninety-eight bottles of beer on the wall,

   Ninety-eight bottles of beer on the wall,
   Ninety-eight bottles of beer . . . *(etc.)*
(They keep singing this softly under the following scene.)
BOO: *(Holding up a piece of paper.)* I pledge, in front of Father Donnally, to give up drinking in order to save my marriage and to make my wife and son happy.
FATHER DONNALLY: Now sign it, Boo.
(Boo signs it.)
BETTE: *(Happy.)* Thank you, Boo. *(Kisses him; to Father Donnally.)* Should you bless him or something?
FATHER DONNALLY: Oh, I don't know. Sure. *(Blesses them.)* In the name of the Father, Son, and Holy Ghost. Amen.
BETTE: Thank you, Father.
FATHER DONNALLY: All problems can be worked out, can't they?
BETTE: Yes, they can.
FATHER DONNALLY: Through faith.
BETTE: And willpower. Boo, let's have another baby.
THOSE SINGING: *(Finishing.)*
   Take one down, pass it around,

God bless us one and all!
(Lights change.)

Scene 20   *Bette and Boo dance. Perhaps no music in the background.*

BETTE: This is fun to go dancing, Boo. We haven't gone since
   before our honeymoon.
BOO: You're mighty pretty tonight, gorgeous.
BETTE: I wonder if Bonnie Wilson grew up to be pretty. We
   were the two stupidest in the class. I don't think Joanie's
   marriage is working out. Nikkos is a louse.
BOO: I think the waiter thought I was odd just ordering ginger
   ale.
BETTE: The waiter didn't think anything about it. You think
   everyone's looking at you. They're not. Emily said she's go-
   ing to pray every day that this baby lives. I wonder what's
   the matter with Emily.
BOO: Your family's crazy.
BETTE: Don't criticize my family, Boo. I'll get angry. Do you
   think I'm prettier than Polly Lydstone?
BOO: Who?
BETTE: You're going to have to make more money when this
   baby comes. I think Father Donnally is very nice, don't you?
   Your father is terrible to your mother. My father was always
   sweet to my mother.
BOO: I think the waiter thinks I'm odd.
BETTE: What is it with you and the waiter? Stop talking about
   the waiter. Let's just have a nice time. *(They dance in si-
   lence.)* Are you having a nice time?
BOO: You're lookin' mighty pretty tonight, Bette.
BETTE: Me too, Boo.
(They dance, cheered up. Lights change.)

Scene 21   *Matt addresses the audience.*

MATT: *Holidays,* an essay by Matthew Hudlocke. Holidays
   were invented in 1203 by Sir Ethelbert Holiday, a sadistic
   Englishman. It was Sir Ethelbert's hope that by setting aside
   specific days on which to celebrate things—the birth of

Christ, the death of Christ, Beowulf's defeat over Grendel—
that the population at large would fall into a collective *deep*
depression. Holidays would regulate joy so that anyone who
didn't feel joyful on those days would feel bad. Single people
would be sad they were single. Married people would be sad
they were married. Everyone would feel disappointment
that their lives had fallen so far short of their expectations.

A small percentage of people, sensing the sadism in Sir
Ethelbert's plan, did indeed pretend to be joyful at these
appointed times; everyone else felt intimidated by this small
group's excessive delight, and so never owned up to being
miserable. And so, as time went on, the habit of celebrating
holidays became more and more ingrained into society.

Eventually humorists like Robert Benchley wrote mildly
amusing essays poking fun at the impossibility of enjoying
holidays, but no one actually spoke up and attempted to
abolish them.

And so, at this time, the Thanksgiving with the gravy
having been such fun, Bette and Boo decide to celebrate the
holiday of Christmas by visiting the Hudlockes.

*(Maybe a bit of Christmas music. Emily sits near Karl and
Soot. Boo is off to one side, drinking something. Bette is off to
another side, looking grim; she is also looking pregnant. Matt
sits on floor near Emily or Soot.)*

EMILY: I think Christmas is becoming too commercial. We
should never forget whose birthday we are celebrating.

SOOT: That's right. Whose birthday are we celebrating?

EMILY: Our Lord Savior.

SOOT: Oh yes, of course. I thought she meant some relative.

EMILY: Jesus.

SOOT: It's so nice of you to visit us today, Emily. I don't think
I've seen you since you were away at that . . . well . . .
away. *(Laughs.)*

EMILY: Skippy asked me to come along, but I'm enjoying it.

KARL: Soot, get Bore and me another drink.

BETTE: IF BOO HAS ANOTHER DRINK, I AM GOING TO
SCREAM AND SCREAM UNTIL THE WINDOWS BREAK!
I WARN YOU! *(Pause.)*

KARL: *(Looks at Bette.)* You're having another baby, woman?

BOO: I told you, Pop. Betsy has a lot of courage.

KARL: You trying to kill Betsy, Bore?

BETTE: I'm going to lie down in the other room. *(To Boo.)* Skippy will tell me if you have another drink. *(Exits.)*

KARL: You sound like quite a scout, Skip. Is Skip a scout, Bore?

BOO: What, Pop?

KARL: Is Skip a scout, Bore?

SOOT: I was a Brownie.

(Re-enter Bette.)

BETTE: Boo upsets Skippy's stomach. *(Sits down.)* I'm not leaving the room. *(Pause.)*

SOOT: *(To Emily.)* My friend Lottie always comes out to visit at Christmastime . . .

KARL: Her friend Lottie looks like an onion.

SOOT: Karl always says she looks like an onion. *(Doing her best.)* But this year Lottie won't be out till after New Year's.

KARL: She may look like an onion, but she smells like a garbage disposal.

SOOT: Oh, Karl. Because this year Lottie slipped on her driveway and broke her hip because of all the ice.

KARL: And she tastes like a septic tank.

SOOT: So when Lottie gets here she's going to have a cast on her . . . Karl, where would they put the cast if you broke your hip?

KARL: Lottie doesn't have hips. She has pieces of raw whale skin wrapped around a septic tank in the middle.

SOOT: Karl doesn't like Lottie.

KARL: That's right.

SOOT: Karl thinks Lottie smells, but I think he's just kidding.

BETTE: HOW CAN YOU SMELL HER WITH ALCOHOL ON YOUR BREATH?

BOO: Oh God.

KARL: What did you say, woman?

BETTE: You're too drunk to smell anything.

BOO: Will you lay off all this drinking talk?

KARL: *(Holds up his drink.)* I think it's time your next stillborn was baptized, don't you, Soot?

SOOT: Karl . . .

(Karl pours his drink on Bette's lap. Bette has hysterics. Lights change.)

Scene 22 *Matt addresses the audience.*

MATT: Twenty years later, Boo has dinner with his son.
(Boo, Matt.)
BOO: Well, how are things up at Dartmouth, Skip? People in
the office ask me how my Ivy League son is doing.
MATT: It's all right.
BOO: Are there any pretty girls up there?
MATT: Uh huh.
BOO: So what are you learning up there?
MATT: Tess of the d'Urbervilles is a . . . I'm not up at Dart-
mouth anymore. I'm at Columbia in graduate school.
BOO: I know that. I meant Columbia. How is it?
MATT: Fine.
BOO: Why are you still going to school?
MATT: I don't know. What do you want me to do?
BOO: I don't know. Your mother and I got divorced, you know.
MATT: Yes, I know. We have discussed this, you know.
BOO: I don't understand why she wanted a divorce. I mean,
we'd been separated for several years, why not just leave it
at that?
MATT: She wants to feel independent, I guess.
BOO: I thought we might get back together. You know, I al-
ways found your mother very charming when she wasn't
shouting. A man needs a woman, son. I think your old man's
going to get teary for a second. Do you have any problems
you want to talk over? *(Blinks his eyes.)* I'm just an old softie.
(Matt steps out of the scene. Boo stays in place.)
MATT: *(To audience.)* At about the same time, Bette also has
dinner with her son.
(Bette, Matt.)
BETTE: Hello, Skippy, dear. I made steak for you, and mashed
potatoes and peas and cake. How many days can you stay?
MATT: I have to get back tomorrow.
BETTE: Can't you stay longer?
MATT: I really have to get back.
BETTE: You never stay long. I don't have much company, you
know. And Polly Lydstone's son goes to her house for dinner
twice a week, and her daughter Mary gave up her apart-

ment and lives at home. And Judith Rankle's son moved home after college and commutes forty minutes to work.

MATT: And some boy from Pingry School came home after class and shot both his parents. So what?

BETTE: There's no need to get nasty.

MATT: I just don't want to hear about Polly Lydstone and Judith Rankle.

BETTE: You're the only one of my children that lived. You should see me more often.

(Matt looks aghast.)

MATT: That's not a fair thing to say.

BETTE: You're right. It's not fair of me to bring up the children that died; that's beside the point. I realize Boo and I must take responsibility for our own actions. Of course, the Church wasn't very helpful at the time, but nonetheless we had brains of our own, so there's no point in assigning blame. I must take responsibility for wanting children so badly that I foolishly kept trying over and over, hoping for miracles. Did you see the article in the paper, by the way, about how they've discovered a serum for people with the Rh problem that would have allowed me to have more babies if it had existed back then?

MATT: Yes, I did. I wondered if you had read about that.

BETTE: Yes, I did. It made me feel terribly sad for a little while; but then I thought, "What's past is past. One has no choice but to accept facts." And I realized that you must live your own life, and I must live mine. My life may not have worked out as I wished, but still I feel a deep and inner serenity, and so you mustn't feel bad about me because I am totally happy and self-sufficient in my pretty sunlit apartment. And now I'm going to close my eyes, and I want you to go out into the world and live your life. Good-bye. God bless you. *(Closes her eyes.)*

MATT: *(To audience.)* I'm afraid I've made that conversation up totally.

(They start the scene over.)

BETTE: Hello, Skippy, dear. I made steak for you, and mashed potatoes and peas and cake. You know, you're the only one of my children that lived. How long can you stay?

MATT: Gee, I don't know. Uh, a couple of days. Three years.

Only ten minutes, my car's double-parked. I could stay eight years if I can go away during the summer. Gee, I don't know. *(Lights change.)*

Scene 23 *Matt addresses the audience.*

MATT: Back in chronology, shortly after the unpleasant Christmas with the Hudlockes, Bette brings Boo back to Father Donnally. *(Matt exits. Bette, Boo, Father Donnally. Bette in a foul temper.)*

BOO: *(Reading.)* I pledge in front of Father Donnally to give up drinking in order to save my marriage and to make my wife and son happy, and this time I mean it.

BETTE: Read the other part.

BOO: *(Reading.)* And I promise to tell my father to go to hell.

FATHER DONNALLY: Oh, I didn't see that part.

BETTE: Now sign it. *(Boo signs it. Crossly, to Father Donnally.)* Now bless us.

FATHER DONNALLY: Oh, all right. In the name of the Father, Son, and Holy Ghost. Amen.

BETTE: Now let's go home. *(Bette and Boo cross to another part of the stage; Father Donnally exits.)* Now if you give up drinking for good this time, maybe God will let this next baby live, Boo.

BOO: Uh huh.

BETTE: And I'm going to go to Mass daily. And Emily is praying.

BOO: Uh huh.

BETTE: You're not very talkative, Boo.

BOO: I don't have anything to say.

BETTE: Well, you should have something to say. Marriage is a fifty-fifty proposition.

BOO: Where do you pick up these sayings? On the back of matchpacks?

BETTE: Why are you being nasty? Have you had a drink already?

BOO: No, I haven't had a drink already. I just find it very humiliating to be constantly dragged in front of that priest all the time so he can hear your complaints about me.

BETTE: You have an idiotic sense of pride. Do you think he

cares what you do? And if you don't want people to know
you drink, then you shouldn't drink.

BOO: You are obsessed with drinking. Were you frightened at
an early age by a drunk? What is the matter with you?

BETTE: What is the matter with *you?*

BOO: What is the matter with *you?*

BETTE: What is the matter with you?

BOO: What is the matter with you?

*(This argument strikes them both funny, and they laugh.
Lights change.)*

Scene 24   *Matt addresses the audience.*

MATT: Shortly after the second pledge, Bette and Skippy visit
the Brennans to celebrate Joanie's birthday. Boo stays home,
drunk or sulking, it's not clear.

*(Margaret, Paul, Bette, Emily, Joan, and Matt. Joan looks preg-
nant; Bette also looks pregnant. Margaret comes downstage
and addresses the audience.)*

MARGARET: All my children live home, it's so nice. Emily's
here, back from the rest home. And Joanie's here because
her marriage hasn't worked out and somebody has to watch
all those children for her while she's working, poor thing.
And Tom's here sometimes, when he gets fired or when his
spastic colon is acting up really badly. Then he always goes
off again, but I bet he ends up here for good eventually!
(Chuckles, pleased.) The only one who hasn't moved back
home is Betsy, because she's so stubborn, but maybe she'll
end up here too someday. I just love having the children
home, otherwise there'd be no one to talk to—unless I
wanted to learn sign language with Paul. *(Laughs.)* Sometimes I'm afraid if I had to choose between having my children succeed in the world and live away from home, or
having them fail and live home, that I'd choose the latter.
But luckily, I haven't had to choose! *(Smiles, returns to the
scene.)* Come on, everybody, let's celebrate Joanie's birthday, and don't anybody mention that she's pregnant with yet
another baby.

BETTE: Every time I look at you, you're using nose spray.

JOAN: You just got here.

Christopher Durang (rest top left clockwise): *Mercedes Ruehl, Joan Allen, Richard B. Shull, Graham Beckel, Bill Moor, Patricia Falkenhain, Olympia Dukakis, Kathryn Grody, Bill McCutcheon*

Bill Moor, Olympia Dukakis, Graham Beckel

Graham Beckel and Joan Allen

Bill McCutcheon, Kathryn Grody, Mercedes Ruehl

BETTE: But the last time I was here. You're going to give your-self a sinus infection.

JOAN: I already have a sinus infection.

MARGARET: The girls always fight. It's so cute. Now, girls.

BETTE: Well, you use too much nose spray. You might hurt the baby inside you.

JOAN: Let's drop the subject of babies, shall we?

BETTE: I can't imagine why you're pregnant again.

EMILY: Happy birthday, Joan! *(Everyone looks at her.)* I made the cake. I better go get it. *(Exits.)*

MARGARET: Where's Booey, Bette?

BETTE: He's home, drunk or sulking, Skippy and I can't decide which. Where's Nikkos, Joan?

JOAN: Under a truck, I hope.

BETTE: Well, you married him. Everyone told you not to.

MARGARET: Let's change the subject. How are you doing in school, Skippy?

MATT: *(Glum.)* Fine.

MARGARET: Isn't that nice?

BETTE: Skippy always gets A's. Is little Mary Frances still getting F's? Maybe if you were home more, she'd do better.

JOAN: I can't afford to be home more. I don't have a life of leisure like you do.

(Enter Emily with the cake.)

EMILY: Happy birthday, Joan.

BETTE: Hush, Emily. If I had several children, I'd *make* time to spend with them.

JOAN: You have a home and a husband, and I don't have either.

BETTE: Well, it's your own fault.

EMILY: Please don't argue, Bette.

BETTE: Why do you say "Bette"? Why not "Joanie"? She's the one arguing.

EMILY: Don't anybody argue.

MARGARET: Don't excite yourself, Emily.

JOAN: You see what your talking has done? You're going to give Emily another breakdown.

EMILY: That's sweet of you to worry, Joanie, but I'm all right.

BETTE: *(To Joan.)* You're just a neurotic mess. You're going to ruin your children.

JOAN: Well, it's lucky you only have one to ruin, or else the mental ward wouldn't have just Emily in it.

(Emily has an asthma attack.)

MARGARET: This cake looks very nice, Emily. Why don't we all have some. I bet Skippy would like a piece.
(Margaret cuts the cake and passes it around.)
EMILY: We forgot to have Joanie blow out the candles.
JOAN: There aren't any candles on the cake.
EMILY: Oh, I forgot them. I'm sorry, Joanie.
JOAN: Why should I have candles? I don't have anything else.
MARGARET: Poor Joanie.
BETTE: The dough's wet. Don't eat it, Skippy, it'll make you sick.
EMILY: It isn't cooked right?
BETTE: It's wet, it's wet. You didn't cook it enough.
JOAN: I don't like cake anyway.
MARGARET: Poor Joanie.
BETTE: Everything's always "poor Joanie." But her baby's going to live.
EMILY: Oh, Bette.
JOAN: Well, maybe we'll both have a miracle. Maybe yours'll live and mine'll die.
EMILY: Oh, Joanie.
BETTE: Stop saying that, Emily.
MARGARET: Girls, girls. This isn't conversation for the living room. Or for young ears.
PAUL: *(Choking on cake.)* # % # % # % GHGHR # % # % # ** - ******* # @ # @ # ********.
MARGARET: Paul, stop it. Stop it.
(Paul falls over dead. Lights change.)

Scene 25 *Matt puts a sheet over Paul and addresses the audience.*

MATT: The funeral of Paul Brennan.
(Paul in a chair with a sheet over him. Present are Matt, Bette, Boo, Margaret, Emily, Joan.)
MARGARET: Paul was a fine husband. Good-bye, Paul. *(Teary.)*
BETTE: Boo, thank you for being sober today. *(Kisses him.)* Look how happy it makes Skippy.
BOO: Skippy's drunk.
BETTE: That's not funny.
(Enter Father Donnally.)
FATHER DONNALLY: Dearly bereaved, Paul Brennan was a

fine man, and now he's dead. I didn't know Paul very well, but I imagine he was a very nice man and everyone spoke well of him. Though he wasn't too able to speak well of them. *(Laughs; everyone looks faintly appalled.)*

It's going to be hard not to miss him, but God put his children on this earth to adapt to circumstances, to do His will.

I was reminded of this fact the other morning, when I saw my colored garbage man collecting the refuse as I was on my way to say Mass. "Good morning, Father," he said. "Nice day." "And what's your name?" I said. "Percival Pretty, Father," he said. I smiled a little more and then I said, "And how are you—Percival?" And he said, "I'm doing the will of God, Father. God saw fit to take my little Buttermilk to Him, and now I'm emptying the garbage." "And who is little Buttermilk?" I said, and he said, "Why, Buttermilk was my daughter who broke her neck playing on the swings." And then he smiled. Colored folk have funny ideas for names. I knew one colored woman who named her daughter "January 22nd." It wasn't easy to forget *her* birthday! *(Everyone looks appalled again.)*

But I think Percival Pretty's smile is a lesson for us all, and so now when I think of Paul Brennan, I'm going to smile. *(Smiles.)* And then nothing can touch you. *(Shakes hands with Margaret.)* Be strong, dear.

EMILY: Thank you, Father, for your talk.

JOAN: *(To Paul's dead body.)* I've turned against Greeks after Nikkos. You were right, Dad, you were right!

MARGARET: Thank you, Joanie. That was a nice gesture.

FATHER DONNALLY: Hello, Bette. Hello, Boo. You're putting on weight, Bette.

BETTE: It's nothing. *(Sadly.)* I mean, it will be nothing.

(Lights change.)

Scene 26   *Matt addresses the audience.*

MATT: Bette goes to the hospital for the fourth time, et cetera, et cetera.

(Matt exits. Karl, Soot, Boo in their hospital "waiting" positions.)

BOO: Pop. Eventually there's menopause, right? I mean, something happens, and then it stops, and . . .

KARL: Where are the Brennans? Have they lost the playing spirit?

BOO: Bette wasn't that way when I married her, was she?

SOOT: Karl, is there still a space between my eyes?

KARL: What did you say, Soot?

SOOT: Nothing. I'll wait till I get home. *(Smiles, feels between her eyebrows.)* Lottie always said when your eyebrows start to kiss, you better watch it.

KARL: Your mother's eyebrows are kissing, Bore.

SOOT: You make everything sound so dirty, Karl. I wish I hadn't said that.

KARL: You want to hear a dirty story? Bore, are you listening? Once there was a traveling salesman, Soot, who met a girl in a barn who was more stupid than you.

SOOT: I don't know this one.

KARL: The girl was an albino. Bore, you listening? She was an albino humpback with a harelip.

BOO: I'm going to get a drink. *(Exits.)*

KARL: And this albino humpback saw the traveling salesman with his dickey hanging out . . .

SOOT: Karl, I have heard this one.

KARL: And she saw his dickey, and she said, "What's that?" and he said, "That's my dickey."

SOOT: Karl, you told this story to Lottie, and she didn't like it.

KARL: And she said, "Why does it swing around like that?" and he said . . . Soot, what's the end of the story?

SOOT: Karl, I never listen to your stories.

KARL: WHAT'S THE ANSWER TO THE JOKE?

SOOT: *(Cries.)* Karl, I don't know. Something about a dickey. Maybe Bore knows. Booey? I have to go home and take a bath. I feel awful. *(Enter the doctor. He drops the baby on the floor, exits. Karl and Soot stare at it a moment.)* Catholics can't use birth control, can they? *(Laughs.)* That's a joke on someone. *(Enter Boo.)*

KARL: You missed it, Boo.

BOO: Did it live?

KARL: Not unless they redefined the term.

SOOT: Don't tease Booey, Karl. Let's distract him, see if he remembers the joke.

KARL: You tell it, Soot.

SOOT: No, I don't like the joke. I just thought maybe he'd remember it.

BOO: It didn't live.

KARL: Tell the joke, Soot.

BOO: Pop, I don't feel like hearing a joke.

SOOT: Poor Booey.

BOO: I should probably see Bette, but I don't think I can face her.

SOOT: Why don't you go get a drink, Booey, you look awful. I've got to go home and check my forehead.

KARL: Tell the damn joke, Soot.

BOO: Pop, I don't want to hear a joke.

SOOT: It's all right, Booey. I'll tell it. Your father seems obsessed with it.

KARL: *(Rams his cigar in her mouth.)* Here, you'll need this.

SOOT: Oh, Karl. *(Laughs.)* All right, Booey, you ready?

BOO: I don't want to hear a joke.

KARL: You'll like it, Bore.

SOOT: Now, Booey . . . *(Boo starts to exit; they follow.)* . . . it seems there was this poor unfortunate, stupid crippled girl, and she met this salesman . . .

BOO: Will you two shut up? I don't want to hear a joke. *(Exits.)*

SOOT: He doesn't want to hear the joke.

KARL: You told it wrong, Soot.

SOOT: I'm sorry, Karl. I'm really not myself today. *(Touches between her eyes.)* I'm sorry, Booey. Booey! *(They exit.)*

Scene 27 *Bette, playing rope or some such thing.*

BETTE:
What is the matter with Mary Jane?
It isn't a cramp, and it isn't a pain,
And lovely rice pudding's for dinner again,
What is the *matter* with Mary Jane?

Christopher Robin had weasles and sneezles,
They bundled him into his bed.
(Kneels, looks at imaginary gravestones; then to audience, sadly.)
The names of the children are: Patrick Michael, February

twenty-sixth; Christopher Tigger, March eighth; and Pooh Bear Eeyore, March twenty-fifth. Bonnie Wilson and I were, were . . . *(Calls.)* Father Donnally! Father Donnally . . . *(Father Donnally enters into Bette's space.)* Father Donnally, can you help me?

FATHER DONNALLY: I'll try. What's on your mind, Bette?

BETTE: I know sometimes one can misunderstand the will of God. But sex is for having babies, right? I mean, it's not just for marriage. Well, even if it is somewhat, I feel that I should be a mother; and I think it would be a sin for me not to try again. But I don't think Boo wants me to get pregnant again.

FATHER DONNALLY: Have you tried the rhythm method?

BETTE: But I *want* to get pregnant.

FATHER DONNALLY: What does your doctor say?

BETTE: The problem is that all the babies die. I don't see why I have to go through all this suffering. And Boo never helps me.

FATHER DONNALLY: I give a retreat for young married couples every year in the parish. Why don't you and your husband come to that? I'm sure it will help you if you're having trouble on the marriage couch.

BETTE: All right, I'll bring Booey to the retreat. Thank you, Father.

FATHER DONNALLY: You're welcome, Bette. *(Father Donnally exits.)*

BETTE: *(Crosses away; calls out.)* Boo. Boo. Booey. Booey. Booey. *(Enter Boo.)*

BOO: What?

BETTE: Booey, I'm pregnant again. Do you think I'm going to die?

(Lights change.)

Scene 28 *The retreat. Present are Bette, Boo; also Margaret, Emily, Joan, the dead Paul (with sheet still over him); Karl, Soot. Enter Father Donnally.*

FATHER DONNALLY: In the name of the Father, of the Son, and of the Holy Ghost, Amen. Good evening, young marrieds. *(Looks about for a moment.)* Am I in the right room?

EMILY: I'm not married, Father. I hope you don't mind that I'm here.

FATHER DONNALLY: On the contrary. I'm delighted. I'm not married either. *(Laughs.)* The theme of marriage in the Catholic Church and in this retreat is centered around the story of Christ and the wedding feast at Cana. Jesus Christ blessed the young wedding couple at Cana, and when they ran out of expensive wine, He performed His first miracle— He took vats of water and He changed the water into wine. *(Holds up a glass.)* I have some wine right here. *(Sips it.)*

BOO: *(To Bette.)* He drinks. Why don't you try to get him to stop drinking?

BETTE: Be quiet, Boo.

FATHER DONNALLY: *(Laughs, nervously.)* Please don't talk when I'm talking. *(Starts his speech.)* Young marrieds have many problems to get used to. For some of them this is the first person of the opposite sex the other has ever known. The husband may not be used to having a woman in his bathroom. The wife may not be used to a strong masculine odor in her boudoir. Or then the wife may not cook well enough. How many marriages have floundered on the rocks of ill-cooked bacon? *(Pause.)* I used to amuse friends by imitating bacon in a saucepan. Would anyone like to see that? *(He looks around. Joan, Karl, and Soot raise their hands. After a moment, Emily, rather confused, raises her hand also. Father Donnally falls to the ground and does a fairly good—or if not good, at least unabashedly peculiar—imitation of bacon, making sizzling noises and contorting his body to represent becoming crisp. Toward the end, he makes sputtering noises into the air. Then he stands up again. All present applaud with varying degrees of approval or incredulity.)* I also do coffee percolating. *(He does this.)* Pt. Pt. Ptptptptptptptpt. Bacon's better. But things like coffee and bacon are important in a marriage, because they represent things that the wife does to make her husband happy. Or fat. *(Laughs.)* The wife cooks the bacon, and the husband brings home the bacon. This is how St. Paul saw marriage, although they probably didn't really eat pork back then, the curing process was not very well worked out in Christ's time, which is why so many of them followed the Jewish dietary laws even though they were Christians. I know I'm glad to be living now when we have cured pork and plumbing and showers rather than back when Christ lived. Many priests say they wish they had lived in Christ's time so they could have met Him; that would, of course, have been very nice, but I'm glad I live now and that I have a shower. *(Emily, bothered by what he's just said, raises her hand.)* I'm not ready for questions yet, Emily. *(Emily lowers her hand; he sips his wine.)* Man and wife, as St. Paul saw it. Now the woman should obey her husband, but that's not considered a very modern thought, so I don't even want to talk about it. All right, don't obey your husbands, but if chaos follows, don't blame me. The tower of Babel as an image of chaos has always fascinated me—

(Emily raises her hand.)

BETTE: Put your hand down, Emily.

(Emily does.)

FATHER DONNALLY: *(To Bette.)* Thank you. Now I don't mean to get off the point. The point is husband and wife, man and woman, Adam and rib. I don't want to dwell on the inequality of the sexes because these vary from couple to couple—sometimes the man is stupid, sometimes the woman is stupid, sometimes both are stupid. The point is man and wife are joined in holy matrimony to complete each other, to populate the earth and to glorify God. That's what it's for. That's what life is for. If you're not a priest or a nun, you normally get married. *(Emily raises her hand.)* Yes, I know, you're not married, Emily. Not everyone gets married. But my comments today are geared toward the *married* people here. *(Emily takes down her hand.)* Man and wife are helpmates. She helps him, he helps her. In sickness and in health. Anna Karenina should not have left her husband, nor should she have jumped in front of a train. Marriage is not a step to be taken lightly. The Church does not recognize divorce; it does permit it, if you insist for legal purposes, but in the eyes of the Church you are still married and you can never be unmarried, and that's why you can never remarry after a divorce because that would be bigamy and that's a sin and illegal as well. *(Breathes.)* So, for God's sake, if you're going to get married, pay attention to what you're doing, have conversations with the person, figure out if you *really* want to live with that person for years and years and years, because you can't change it. Priests have it easier. If I don't like my pastor, I can apply for a transfer. If I don't like a housekeeper, I can get her fired. *(Looks disgruntled.)* But a husband and wife are *stuck* together. So know what you're doing when you get married. I get so *sick* of these people coming to me after they're married, and they've just gotten to know one another *after* the ceremony, and they've discovered they have nothing in common and they hate one another. And they want me to come up with a solution. *(Throws up his hands.)* What can I do? There is no solution to a problem like that. I can't help them! It puts me in a terrible position. I can't say get a divorce, that's against God's law. I can't say go get some on the side, that's against God's law. I can't say just pretend you're happy and maybe after a while you won't know the difference because, though that's not against God's law, not that many people know how to do that, and if I suggested it to people, they'd write to the Bishop complaining about me and then he'd transfer me to some godforsaken place in Latin America without a shower, and all because these people don't know what they're doing when they get married. *(Shakes his head.)* So I mumble platitudes to these people who come to me with these insoluble problems, and I think to myself, "Why didn't they *think* before they got married? Why does no one ever *think?* Why did God make people stupid?" *(Pause.)* Are there any questions?

(Bette raises her hand, as does Emily. Father acknowledges Bette.)

BETTE: Father, if I have a little girl rather than a boy, do you think it might live? Should I pray for this?

FATHER DONNALLY: You mean . . . a little girl to clean house?

BETTE: *(Irritated.)* No. I don't mean a little girl to clean house. I mean that the doctors say that sometimes a little girl baby fights infection better than a little boy baby, and that maybe if I have a little girl baby, the fighting between the Rh positive blood in her body and the Rh negative blood in my body would not destroy her, and she might live. *(Pause.)* Should I pray for this?

FATHER DONNALLY: By all means, pray for it. Just don't get your hopes up too high, though, maybe God doesn't want you to have any more babies. It certainly doesn't sound like it to me.

BETTE: But I *can* pray?

FATHER DONNALLY: Yes. You can. No one can stop you.

BETTE: That's what I thought.

(Emily raises her hand.)

FATHER DONNALLY: *(Dreading whatever she's going to say.)* Yes, Emily?

EMILY: Do you think maybe it's my fault that all of Bette's babies die? Because I left the convent?

FATHER DONNALLY: Yes, I do.

EMILY: *(Stricken.)* Oh my God.

FATHER DONNALLY: I'm sorry, Emily, I was just kidding. Are there any questions about newly married couples? *(Pause; no one stirs.)* Well, I don't have time for any more questions anyway. We'll take a short break for refreshments, and then Father McNulty will talk to you about sexual problems, which I'm not very good at, and then you can all go home. Thank you for your attention. In the name of the Father, and of the Son, and of the Holy Ghost. Amen. *(Starts to exit.)*

EMILY: Father . . .

FATHER DONNALLY: I was just kidding, Emily, I am sorry. Excuse me, I have to go to the bathroom. *(Exits in a hurry.)*

JOAN: You know, he makes a better piece of bacon than he does a priest.

EMILY: I don't think he should joke about something like that.

MARGARET: He's a priest, Emily.

EMILY: I know you're right, Mom, but everyone should want to meet Our Savior, that's more important than having a shower . . .

MARGARET: Don't talk anymore, Emily.

BETTE: Did that make you feel better, Boo? Are you going to be easier to live with?

BOO: *(Sarcastic.)* Yes, it's all better now.

BETTE: Why won't you let anyone help us?

BOO: What help? He just said that we shouldn't get married, and that if we did, not to bother him with our problems.

BETTE: That's not what he said at all.

MARGARET: Bette, don't talk anymore. Hello, Mrs. Hudlocke. Did you enjoy the talk?

SOOT: I'm sorry, what?

MARGARET: Did you enjoy Father's talk?

SOOT: You know, I can't hear you. I think I'm going deaf. God, I hope so.

MARGARET: What do you mean?

SOOT: I'm sorry, I really can't hear you. *(Laughs.)* I haven't been able to hear Karl for about three days. *(Laughs.)* It's wonderful.

BETTE: You should see an ear specialist.

SOOT: What?

BETTE: Oh, never mind.

EMILY: Mom, don't you think . . .

MARGARET: Emily, I said not to talk.

BETTE: Well, if you don't want us to talk, what do you want us to do?

MARGARET: Don't be cranky, Betsy. We'll just all wait for Father McNulty. Maybe he'll have something useful to say.

(They all wait. Soot smiles.)

SOOT: *(To audience.)* Little blessings. *(Laughs. Lights change.)*

Scene 29   *Matt addresses the audience. Bette, Boo, and the dead Paul stay onstage.*

MATT: Twenty years later, or perhaps only fifteen, Bette files for a divorce from Boo. They have been separated for several years, since shortly after the death of the final child; and at the suggestion of a therapist Bette has been seeing, Bette decides to make the separation legal in order to formalize the breakup psychologically, and also to get better, and more regular, support payments. Boo, for some reason, decides to contest the divorce; and so there has to be testimony. Margaret and Joanie decide that Catholics can't testify in divorce cases, even though Bette had eventually testified in Joanie's divorce; and so they refuse to testify, frightening Emily into agreeing with them also. Blah blah blah, et cetera. So in lieu of other witnesses, I find myself sort of having to testify against Boo during my sophomore year at college. I am trying to work on a paper on Thomas Hardy, but find it difficult to concentrate. I fly home for the divorce proceedings. My mother's lawyer reminds me of my grandfather Paul.

(Bette and Boo on opposite sides. Matt, center, testifies, questioned by Paul who comes to life with no to-do. He still speaks in Paul's incomprehensible speech, but otherwise is quite lawyerly.)

PAUL: Ehl ee att, oo## oou ing orr agh##er uz acgh acgha@@lehc? [Tell me, Matt, do you think your father was an alcoholic?]

MATT: What?

PAUL: *(Irritated he can't be understood, as Paul used to be.)* Oo## oou ing, orr agh##er uz acgh acgha@@lehc? [Do you think your father was an alcoholic?]

MATT: Yes, I do feel he drank a fair amount.

PAUL: Uht us ee acgh acgha@@lehc? [But was he an alcoholic?]

MATT: I'm really not in the position to say if anyone is actually an alcoholic or not.

BETTE: I have a calendar here from the twelve years of our marriage. Every time it says "HD," that stands for "half-drunk." And everytime it says "DD," that stands for "dead drunk." I offer this as Exhibit A.

PAUL: *(Telling her it's not her turn.)* Eeez own awk enn oo aht ahn uh ann. [Please don't talk when you're not on the stand.]

BETTE: What?

BOO: I was never dead drunk. She has this thing about drunks.

MATT: *(To Bette.)* He said you shouldn't talk when you're not on the stand.

BETTE: I didn't.

PAUL: *(To Bette.)* Ssssh. *(Long question to Matt.)* Ehl ee att, ihd oo## eheh ee or ah#er ah ehey ohazsn, itt or uher? [Tell me, Matt, did you ever see your father, on any occasion, hit your mother?]

MATT: Yes. Hardy wrote *Tess of the d'Urbervilles* in 1891.

PAUL: *(Irritated.)* As ott ut uh ass. [That's not what I asked.]

MATT: Oh, I'm sorry. I misheard the question.

PAUL: Ihd ee itt er? [Did he hit her?] *(Makes hitting motion.)*

MATT: Yes, I did see him hit her.

PAUL: Ah!

MATT: Of course, she hit him too. They both hit each other. Especially when they were driving. It was fairly harrowing from the back seat.

BETTE: He started it.

BOO: She'd talk and talk like it was a sickness. There was no way of shutting her up.

MATT: Well, I would have appreciated your not arguing when you were driving a car.

PAUL: *(To Bette and Boo.)* Ee i###et! [Be quiet!]

MATT: Or at least left me home.

PAUL: Shhh! *(Back to questioning Matt.)* Ehl ee att, oo oo# ih or ohn lhahf eher agh uh ink? [Tell me, Matt, do you in your own life ever have a drink?]

MATT: No, I don't know any happily married couples. Certainly not relatives.

PAUL: *(Irritated.)* As ott ut uh ass. [That's not what I asked.]

MATT: Oh, I'm sorry. I thought that's what you asked.

PAUL: Oo oo# ih or ohn lhahf eher agh uh ink? [Do you in your own life ever have a drink?]

MATT: No, my paper is on whether Eustacia Vye in *The Return of the Native* is neurotic or psychotic, and how she compares to Emily. That isn't what you asked either, is it? I'm sorry. What?

PAUL: *Oo oo# ink?* [Do you drink?]

MATT: Ink?

PAUL: *(Gesturing as if drinking.)* Ink! Ink!

MATT: No, I don't drink, actually.

PAUL: Ehl ee att, urr oo uhaagee ehn or errens epyrateted? [Tell me, Matt, were you unhappy when your parents separated?]

(Matt is at a loss. Paul must repeat the word "separated" several times, with hand gestures, before Matt understands.)

MATT: No, I was glad when they separated. The arguing got on my nerves a lot. *(Pause.)* I'd hear it in my ear even when they weren't talking. When I was a child, anyway.

PAUL: Ehl ee att, oo oo# ink or aher uz uh goooh aher? [Tell me, Matt, do you think your father was a good father?]

MATT: Yes, I am against the war in Vietnam. I'm sorry, is that what you asked?

PAUL: Doo oo# ink ee uz a goooh ahzer? [Do you think he was a good father?]

MATT: Oh. Yes. I guess he's been a good father. *(Looks embarrassed.)*

PAUL: *(Pointing at Boo, pushing for some point.)* Buh dyoo oo# ink ee ad ohme or uh inkng bahblim? [But do you think he had some sort of drinking problem?] *(Makes drinking gesture.)*

MATT: Yes, I guess he probably does have some sort of drinking problem. *(Becoming worked up.)* I mean it became such an issue it seems suspicious to me that he didn't just stop, he kept saying there was no . . . *(Pulls back.)* Well, it was odd

he didn't stop. It's really not my place to be saying this. I would prefer I wasn't here.
(Pause. Matt is uncomfortable, has been uncomfortable relating to Boo for the whole scene.)
PAUL: Orr ehcoooz, att. [You're excused, Matt.]
MATT: What?
BETTE: He said you were excused.
MATT: Oh good.
(Paul exits, or goes back under sheet.)
BETTE: Thank you, Skippy. *(Kisses him.)*
BOO: Well, son. Have a good time back at school.
MATT: Thank you. I'm behind in this paper I'm doing. *(Pause.)* I have to get the plane.
BOO: Well, have a good trip. *(Looks embarrassed, exits.)*
MATT: Thank you. *(Bette exits. Matt addresses the audience.)* Eustacia Vye is definitely neurotic. Whether she is psychotic as well is . . . In *Return of the Native,* Hardy is dealing with some of the emotional, as well as physical, dangers in the . . . One has to be very careful in order to protect oneself from the physical and emotional dangers in the world. One must always be careful crossing streets in traffic. One should try not to live anywhere near a nuclear power plant. One should never walk past a building that may have a sniper on top of it. In the summer one should be on the alert against bees and wasps.

As to emotional dangers, one should always try to avoid crazy people, especially in marriage or live-in situations, but in everyday life as well. Although crazy people often mean well, meaning well is not enough. On some level Attila the Hun may have meant well.

Sometimes it is hard to decide if a person is crazy, like Eustacia Vye in *The Return of the Native,* which is the topic of this paper. Some people may seem sane at first, and then at some later point turn out to be totally crazy. If you are at dinner with someone who suddenly seems insane, make up some excuse why you must leave the dinner immediately. If they don't know you well, you can say you're a doctor and pretend that you just heard your beeper. If the crazy person should call you later, either to express anger at your abrupt leave-taking or to ask for medical advice, claim the connection is bad and hang up. If they call back, I'm afraid you'll have to have your phone number changed again. When you call the phone company to arrange this, if the person on the line seems stupid, hostile, or crazy, simply hang up and call the phone company back again. This may be done as many times as necessary *until you get someone sane.* As the phone company has many employees. *(Breathes.)* It is difficult to totally protect oneself, of course, and there are many precautions that one thinks of only when it's too late. But, as Virginia Woolf pointed out in *To the Lighthouse,* admittedly in a different context, the attempt is all.

Sometime after the divorce, five years or fifteen or something, Skippy has dinner with Karl and Soot and Margaret and Paul. Karl is near eighty, Margaret is senile, and Paul and Soot are dead.

Scene 30 *Matt sits at a table with all four. Paul and Soot have their heads on the table, dead. Karl seems fairly normal and himself; Margaret is distracted and vague.*

MATT: Hello. Nice to see you all.
MARGARET: Emily! Huh-huh-huh. Tom! Nurse! Huh-huh-huh. (NOTE: *the "huh-huh-huh" sound is not like laughter, but is a nervous tic, said softly and rather continuously throughout the scene. Technically speaking, it's like a mild vocal exercise using the diaphragm, like an ongoing cough reflex with no real cough behind it. A tic.)*
KARL: You're Skip, aren't you?
MATT: Yes. You remember me?
KARL: Yes, I remember you.
MARGARET: Doctor. Mama. Huh-huh-huh. Huh-huh-huh.
KARL: *(To Margaret.)* Shut up.
MATT: *(To Karl, with seriousness.)* What do you think I should do with my life?
KARL: Well, don't marry Soot.
MATT: Yes, but you know—
MARGARET: Emily! Huh-huh-huh.
MATT: Everyone I know is divorced except for you and Soot, and Margaret and Paul. Of course, Soot and Paul are dead, but you all stayed married right up until death. And I wondered what mistakes you thought I could avoid based on all your experience.
KARL: Don't expect much, that's for starters. Look at Bette

and Bore. She kept trying to change Bore. That's idiotic.
Don't try to change anybody. If you don't like them, be
mean to them if you want; try to get them committed if that
amuses you, but don't ever expect to *change* them.
(Matt considers this.)
MATT: Do you agree with that, Grandma?
MARGARET: *(Seeing Matt for the first time, leaning over to
him.)* Go to the baperdy sun ride zone a bat.
MATT: Baperdy?
MARGARET: Lamin fortris trexin home. Emily!
KARL: It's too bad Paul's not still alive. It would be interesting
to hear them talk together now.
(Matt laughs at this.)
MATT: Grandma, try to be lucid. I think Karl's advice makes
sense, sort of, if you're in a bad marriage. But what if you're
not in a bad marriage?
MARGARET: When the bob?
MATT: I said, do you agree with Karl? Or do you see something
more optimistic?
MARGARET: I want Emily to clean the mirrors with milk of
magnesia. I see people in the mirrors and they don't go
away.
KARL: At least that was a complete sentence.
MATT: Emily's not here right now.
MARGARET: Everyone's so late. Dabble morning hunting
back, Emily. Huh-huh-huh.
MATT: *(Gives up on Margaret; back to Karl.)* You know, I
didn't know you and Soot back when you were young, or
Margaret and Paul either, for that matter. Maybe your mar-
riages *were* happy. I have no way of knowing.
KARL: I never expected much from life. I wanted to get my
way in everything, and that's about all. What did you ask?
MARGARET: Huh-huh-huh. Joan. Emily.
MATT: Why did you marry Soot?
KARL: No reason. She was much prettier when she was
younger.
MATT: But surely you didn't marry her because she was pretty.
KARL: Don't tell me what I did.
MATT: And why did everyone call her Soot? How did she get
the name "Soot"?
KARL: I don't remember. Was her name Soot? I thought it was
something else.

MATT: I think her name was Soot. Do you think I misheard it all these years?

KARL: I couldn't say.

MATT: Why were you so mean to Soot?

KARL: Why do you want to know?

MATT: Because I see all of you do the same thing over and over, for years and years, and you never change. And my fear is that I can see all of you but not see myself, and maybe I'm doing something similar, but I just can't see it. What I mean to say is: did you all *intend* to live your lives the way you did?

KARL: Go away. I don't like talking to you. You're an irritating young man.

(Matt leaves the scene. Karl, Margaret, Soot, and Paul exit or fade into darkness.)

Scene 31

MATT: *(Trying to find his place. To audience.)* Back into chronology again. Bette had the first baby, that is, the first dead baby, in 1951 or something. And then the second one in 1953 or 4 or something, and then . . . *(Enter Emily.)*

EMILY: Hello, Skippy, dear. How does this sound to you? *(Reads from a note.)* "Please forgive my annoying qualities. I know that I talk too much about a thing and that I make people nervous that I do so. I am praying that I improve that fault and beg that you be patient with me."

MATT: Who is that to, Emily?

EMILY: I don't know. Who do you think it should be to?

MATT: I don't know. It would be up to you.

EMILY: Do you think it's all right?

MATT: I don't think you should be so hard on yourself, but otherwise I think it's fine.

EMILY: Oh, thank you. *(Exits.)*

MATT: Okay. Just as dreams must be analyzed, so must the endless details of waking life be considered.

Having intelligence allows one to analyze problems and to make sense of one's life. This is difficult to achieve, but with perseverance and persistence it is possible not even to get up in the morning. To sleep. "To sleep, perchance to dream," to take the phone off the hook and simply be unreachable. This is less *dramatic* than suicide, but more *reversible.*

I can't make sense out of these things anymore. Um, Bette goes to the hospital for the third time, and there's the second dead baby, and then the fourth time, and the third dead baby, and then sometime after Father Donnally's marriage retreat, Bette goes to the hospital for the fifth time. The *last* child of Bette and Boo.

Scene 32   *Enter Boo. He and Matt are in their "waiting" positions back in the hospital.*

BOO: You don't have to wait here, Skip, if you don't want.
MATT: It's all right.
BOO: Who knows, maybe it will live. The doctors say if it's a girl, girls sometimes fight harder for life. Or something. *(Pause.)* You doing well in school?
MATT: Uh huh.
(The doctor throws the baby, in a pink blanket, in from offstage.)
DOCTOR: *(Offstage.)* It was a girl.
BOO: You have any problems you want to talk over, son? Your old man could help you out.
MATT: I'll be outside a minute. *(Exits. Enter Bette.)*
BOO: Bette, let's not have any more. *(Mournfully.)* I've had enough babies. They get you up in the middle of the night, dead. They dirty their cribs, dead. They need constant attention, dead. No more babies.
BETTE: I don't love you anymore, Boo.
BOO: What?
BETTE: Why do you say what? Can't you hear?
BOO: Why do they never have a bar in this hospital? Maybe there's one on another floor.
BETTE: I'm tired of feeling alone talking to you.
BOO: Maybe I'll take the elevator to another floor and check.
BETTE: They don't have bars in hospitals, Boo.
BOO: I think I'll walk down. See you later. *(Exits.)*
BETTE: I feel alone, Boo. Skippy, are you there? Skippy?
(Enter Matt.)
MATT: Yes.
BETTE: Would you move this for me? *(She indicates dead baby*

on floor. He gingerly places it offstage.) Your father's gone away. All the babies are dead. You're the only thing of value left in my life, Skippy.

MATT: Why do you call me "Skippy"? Why don't you call me "Matt"?

BETTE: It's my favorite movie.

MATT: *(With growing anger.)* My favorite movie is *Citizen Kane.* I don't call you "Citizen Kane."

BETTE: Why are you being fresh?

MATT: I don't know.

BETTE: I don't want to put any pressure on you, Skippy, dear, but you're the only reason I have left for living now.

MATT: Ah.

BETTE: You're so unresponsive.

MATT: I'm sorry. I don't know what to say.

BETTE: You're a typical Capricorn, cold and ungiving. I'm an Aries, we like fun, we do three things at once. We make life decisions by writing our options on little pieces of paper and then throwing them up in the air and going "Wheeee!" Wee wee wee, all the way home. I should have had more babies, I'm very good with babies. Babies *give* to you, then they grow up and they don't give. If I'd had more, I wouldn't mind as much. I don't mean to be critical, it's just that I'm so very . . . *(Looks sad, shakes her head.)* I need to go to bed. Come and read to me from A. A. Milne until I fall asleep, would you?

MATT: All right.

(Bette starts to leave.)

BETTE: *(Suddenly tearful.)* I don't want to call you "Matt."

MATT: That's all right. It's fine. I'll be in to read to you in a minute, okay?

BETTE: Okay. *(Bette exits.)*

MATT: So I read her to sleep from *The House at Pooh Corner.* And then I entered high school, and then I went to college, and then they got divorced, and then I went to graduate school. I stopped studying Thomas Hardy for a while and tried Joseph Conrad. Oh, the horror, the horror. I'm afraid what happened next will sound rather exaggerated, but after she divorced Boo, Bette felt very lonely and unhappy for several years, and then she married another alcoholic, and then after two years that broke up, and then she got cancer.

By this time I'm thirty, and I visit her once more in the hospital.

Scene 33 *Emily pushes Bette on in a wheelchair. Bette doesn't look well.*

EMILY: Doesn't Bette look well today?

MATT: Very well.

EMILY: Let's join hands. *(Holds Matt and Bette's hands.)* In the name of the Father, and of the Son, and of the Holy Ghost, Amen. Heavenly Father, please lift this sickness from our beloved Bette. We place ourselves in Your hands. Amen. *(To Bette.)* Do you feel any better?

BETTE: The pain is a little duller.

EMILY: Well, maybe I better go to the hospital chapel and pray some more.

BETTE: That would be nice, Emily. Thank you. *(Emily exits.)* I've spent a lot of time in hospitals.

MATT: Yes.

BETTE: I sometimes wonder if God is punishing me for making a second marriage outside the Church. But Father Ehrhart says that God forgives me, and besides the second marriage is over now anyway.

MATT: I don't think God punishes people for specific things.

BETTE: That's good.

MATT: I think He punishes people in general, for no reason.

BETTE: *(Laughs.)* You always had a good sense of humor, Skippy. The chemotherapy hasn't been making my hair fall out after all. So I haven't needed those two wigs I bought. The woman at Lord and Taylor's looked at me so funny when I said I needed them because my hair was going to fall out. Now *she* didn't have a good sense of humor. Emily brought me this book on healing, all about these cases of people who are very ill and then someone prays over them and places their hand on the place where the tumor is, and there's this feeling of heat where the tumor is, and then the patient gets completely cured. Would you pray over me, and place your hand on my hip?

MATT: I'm afraid I don't believe in any of that.

BETTE: It won't kill you to try to please me.

MATT: All right. *(Puts his hand on her hip.)*

BETTE: Now say a prayer.

MATT: *(Said quickly as befits a parochial school childhood.)* Hail Mary, full of grace, the Lord is with thee. Blessed art thou amongst women, and blessed is the fruit of thy womb, Jesus. Holy Mary, mother of God, pray for us sinners, now and at the hour of our death, amen.

BETTE: I think I feel a warmth there.

MATT: *(Noncommittal.)* That's good.

BETTE: You're so cold, you won't give anything.

MATT: If I don't believe in prayer, you shouldn't make me pray. It feels funny.

BETTE: You're just like your father—unresponsive.

MATT: Let's not argue about this.

BETTE: All right. *(On a pleasanter subject.)* Do you remember when you used to smell your father's breath to see if he'd been drinking? You were such a cute child. I saw your father last week. He came to the hospital to visit.

MATT: Oh, how is he?

BETTE: Well, he's still mad at me about my second marriage, but in some ways he's always been a sweet man. I think the years of drinking have done something to his brain, though. He'll be talking and then there'll be this long pause like he's gone to sleep or something, and then finally he'll go on again like nothing's happened.

(Enter Boo, holding flowers.)

BOO: Bette?

BETTE: Oh, Boo, I was just talking about you. Look, Skippy's here.

BOO: Oh, Skip. How are you?

MATT: I'm fine. Hi. How are you?

BOO: You look good.

MATT: Oh yes? Do you want a chair?

BOO: What?

MATT: I'll get you a chair. *(He does.)*

BOO: Skip looks good.

BETTE: Yes.

MATT: Do you want to sit? *(Boo looks uncomprehending.)* I've brought you a chair.

BOO: Oh, thank you. *(Sits.)*

BETTE: The flowers are lovely.

BOO: I brought you flowers.

BETTE: Thank you. *(Boo hands them to her.)*

BOO: *(To Matt.)* Your mother still looks very pretty.

MATT: Mother said you came to visit last week.

BOO: I came last week.

BETTE: He repeats himself all the time.

BOO: What?

BETTE: I said, you repeat yourself. *(Boo looks annoyed.)* But it's charming. *(To Matt.)* Your father flirted with the second-shift nurse.

BOO: Your old man still has an eye for the ladies. I was here last week and there was this . . . *(Long pause; he stares, blank.)*

BETTE: *(To Matt.)* See, he's doing it now. Boo, are you there? Boo? *(Sings to herself.)* God bless Bette and Boo and Skippy, Emily and Boo . . .

BOO: *(Comes back, continues.)* . . . nurse, and she liked your old man, I think.

BETTE: She thought he was her grandfather.

BOO: What?

BETTE: You're too old for her.

BOO: What?

MATT: Maybe he's gone deaf.

BOO: No, I can hear. I think it's my brain.

BETTE: Do you remember when you tried to vacuum the gravy?

BOO: No.

BETTE: Well, you did. It was very funny. Not at the time, of course. And how you used to keep bottles hidden in the cellar. And all the dead babies.

BOO: *(Smiles, happy.)* Yes. We had some good times.

BETTE: Yes, we did. And do you remember that time after we got divorced when I came by your office because Mrs. Wright died?

MATT: Mrs. Wright?

BETTE: You were at college, and I didn't have her very long. She was a parakeet. *(Matt suddenly comprehends with an "ah" or "oh" sound.)* And I called her Mrs. Wright because she lived in a Frank Lloyd Wright birdcage, I think. Actually it was a male parakeet but I liked the name better. Anyway, I kept Mrs. Wright free on the screen porch, out of the cage, because she liked it that way, but she'd always try to follow me to the kitchen, so I'd have to get to the porch door before Mrs. Wright, and I always did. Except this one time, we had a tie, and I squashed Mrs. Wright in the door. Mary Roberts

Rinehart wrote a novel called *The Door*, but I like her *Tish* stories better. Well, I was very upset, and it almost made me wish I was still married to Boo so he could pick it up. So I went to Boo's office and I said, "Mrs. Wright is lying on the rug, squashed, come help," and he did. *(To Boo, with great affection.)* You were very good. *(To Matt.)* But then I think he went out and got drunk.

BOO: I remember that parakeet.

MATT: *(To Boo.)* Why did you drink? *(To Bette.)* Why did you keep trying to have babies? Why didn't Soot leave Karl? Why was her name "Soot"?

BETTE: I don't know why her name was "Soot." I never had a parakeet that talked. I even bought one of those records that say "Pretty blue boy, pretty blue boy," but it never picked it up. Boo picked Mrs. Wright up. As a joke, I called people up and I played the record over the phone, pretty blue boy, pretty blue boy; and people kept saying, "Who is this?" Except Emily, she tried to have a conversation with the record.

BOO: I remember that parakeet. You shut the door on it.

BETTE: We moved past that part of the story, Boo. Anyway, then I called Bonnie Wilson and I played the record for her, and she knew it was me right away, she didn't even have to ask. It's nice seeing your parents together again, isn't it, Skippy?

MATT: *(Taken aback, but then it is nice.)* Yes, very nice.

BOO: *(To Matt.)* I was just remembering when you were a little boy, Skip, and how very thrilled your mother and I were to have you. You had all this hair on your head, a lot of hair for a baby; we thought, "We have a little monkey here," but we were very happy to have you, and I said to your mother . . . *(Pause; he has another blackout; stares . . .)*

BETTE: Ooops, there he goes again. Boo? Boo? *(Feels pain.)* I better ring for the nurse. I need a shot for pain.

MATT: Should I go?

BETTE: No. Wait till the nurse comes.

BOO: *(Coming back.)* . . . to your mother, "Where do you think this little imp of a baby came from?"

BETTE: We finished that story, Boo.

BOO: Oh.

MATT: I do need to catch my train.

BETTE: Stay a minute. I feel pain. It'll go in a minute.

(Matt smiles, looks away, maybe for the nurse. Bette closes her eyes, and is motionless.)

BOO: Bette? Betsy?

MATT: Is she sleeping?

(Matt, with some hesitation, feels for a pulse in her neck. Enter Emily.)

EMILY: Oh, hello, Boo. It's nice to see you. Are you all right, Skippy?

MATT: She died, Emily.

EMILY: Then she's with God. Let's say a prayer over her.

(Emily and Boo pray by Bette's body. Music to "Bette and Boo" theme is heard softly. Matt speaks to the audience.)

MATT: Bette passed into death, and is with God. She is in heaven, where she has been reunited with the four dead babies, and where she waits for Boo, and for Bonnie Wilson, and Emily, and Pooh Bear and Eeyore, and Kanga and Roo; and for me.

(Lights dim. End of play.)

AUTHOR'S NOTES

I feel particularly close to *The Marriage of Bette and Boo*, and to the excellent production the play received this past spring at Joseph Papp's New York Shakespeare Festival.

The play itself has a rather long history. I wrote the first draft of the play—a forty-five-minute, one-act version—when I was still a student at Yale School of Drama, and it was produced there my final year (1974).

The play had the same characters and the same number of stillborn children, but otherwise was much more sketchlike, and its emotional impact was far more elliptical. For instance, the scene at Thanksgiving, Bette's phone call, Matt's dinner with the dead grandparents, the divorce scene, the final hospital scene—all these were not in this early version.

The one-act version received a very good student production, directed by Bill Ludel, and featured (among others) Kate McGregor-Stewart as Bette, John Rothman as Boo, Franchelle Stewart Dorn as Emily, Walton Jones as Father Donnally, and Sigourney Weaver as Soot.

At Yale my work had been controversial up to this point, especially *Better Dead Than Sorry*, which featured Sigourney Weaver singing the title song while receiving shock treatments. *Bette and Boo*, though, seemed to win over a far larger audience to my work (at Yale, that is), and was said to have more of a sense of compassion in the midst of the dark humor.

There were subsequently four other productions (that I know of) of the one-act version. The first was at Williamstown Theatre's Second Company, directed by Peter Schifter. I didn't see this production, but heard positive reports, and was especially gratified to hear it was a big success when presented at a women's prison where the inmates apparently got into cheering on Bette and, well, booing Boo.

Then there was a summer Yale cabaret version, directed by

Walton Jones, and featuring Christine Estabrook as Bette, Charles Levin as Boo, and (ah-hem) Meryl Streep as bitter sister Joan. Then a workshop at Chicago's St. Nicholas Theatre Company (now closed, and lamented). And finally a Princeton College undergraduate production, directed by Mitchell Ivers, and with actress-writer Winnie Holzman as a memorable, giggling Soot.

Around 1976, I decided not to let the one-act version be performed anymore, because I felt that the material could be expanded to full-length, and I wanted to hold off wider exposure of the work until I did that.

The play "feels" autobiographical, I rather assume; and it would be disingenuous to pretend that the characters of Bette and Boo do not in many significant ways reflect my parents' lives. Many of the surrounding characters and events are indeed fictionalized, but there is a core to the play that is pretty much rooted in my past.

I wrote the first "expansion" of the play sometime in 1980, and had a reading of it at the Actors Studio. Having met Joseph Papp a few times by then, I called him up and asked him if I could arrange a reading of the play for him—which I did. From that reading, I did various rewrites, especially relating to Father Donnally, and to the character of Matt, which was almost nonexistent in the one-act version.

For complicated reasons, the play kept not being scheduled over the next couple years, though it never died at the Public, thanks to Papp's interest, and to the support of Gail Merrifield and Bill Hart in the play department, and of others there as well (Robert Blacker, Lynn Holst, John Ferraro, Morgan Jenness).

In the summer of 1984, Papp and I agreed upon Jerry Zaks as director, and the play was scheduled for the 1984–85 season. Zaks, as original director of *Sister Mary Ignatius, Beyond Therapy* (off-Broadway), and *Baby with the Bathwater,* had clearly become somewhat of a specialist in doing my work, and our familiarity with one another has made for that wonderful ease and shorthand that sometimes happens with a long-term collaboration.

Mr. Papp (I do call him Joe, but Catholic schoolboy manners are hard to break) was very much of the opinion that I should play the part of Matt myself. Just as Tom in *The Glass Menagerie* "feels" like an author surrogate, so does the part of Matt;

and Papp, who had seen me perform a few times, felt that my doing the role was a head-on way of dealing with the "author's voice" nature of the part that might pay off.

I was fearful that it might seem self-indulgent or self-pitying to have me play Matt; but conversely I also thought it might work fine, and I had had success sometimes acting in my own plays at Yale (though never in parts that had any biographical reverberations). Plus, I thought that if I were to turn down the chance, I would always wonder what it might have been like. So, particularly since Zaks was to be at the helm, I chose to chance it. (I did tell Jerry before rehearsals that I wouldn't hate him if he decided it wasn't working and I should be replaced.)

Performing the role, particularly in previews when it was very new, sometimes struck me as a preposterously public manner in which to reveal some rather personal thoughts and feelings. Since I don't feel I'm easily open about emotions to begin with, it seemed terribly odd to me that I had gotten myself into this position.

Most of the feedback I got on my doing the part was extremely positive; and I know that the last scene in particular, as experienced from inside it (and shared with actors Joan Allen, Graham Beckel, and Kathryn Grody), seemed suffused with a sense of letting go and finishing that acknowledged anger but ended, basically, with—well, I was going to say with acceptance and love, but that sounds glib and rhythmically convenient. But then that probably is what I mean. I know that acting the last scene did feel extremely positive and not at all despairing (though certainly sadness was there).

Some people, I'm told, dismiss this play as too angry; I don't agree with them and feel they may be denying something I've found to be true: that unless you go through all the genuine angers you feel, both justified and unjustified, the feelings of love that you do have will not have any legitimate base and will be at least partially false. Plus, eventually you will go crazy. Well, anyway, I'm glad I wrote the expanded version and that I played Matt.

The production of *The Marriage of Bette and Boo* at the Public Theatre was the most positive and joyful experience I have had in professional theater up to this point (and I say that having liked most of my theatrical experiences). The pleasure of working with Jerry Zaks again, total agreement with all three designers, the support of all the departments in Papp's excellent New York Shakespeare Festival—this made for a production experience with no drawbacks. I may sound gaga with praise, but it would be pointless not to acknowledge it.

As for the actors, I've usually felt fondness and admiration for all the casts I've worked with, but the *Bette and Boo* company grew to be an especially close and loving one.

The ten parts are of varying size, of course, but each part is rather meaty in its way; and a few days after our opening in early May, all ten of us shared in an Obie award for Ensemble Acting. The "Ensemble," as we grew fond of grandly calling ourselves, consisted of Joan Allen, Graham Beckel, Olympia Dukakis, Patricia Falkenhain, Kathryn Grody, Bill McCutcheon, Bill Moor, Mercedes Ruehl, Richard B. Shull, and myself. God bless us, each and every one.

I also won an Obie for playwriting, Jerry Zaks for direction (and for his direction of Larry Shue's *The Foreigner),* and Loren Sherman for his set designs over the past couple of seasons, including *Bette and Boo.* One wants to limit how important awards and critical praise seem for all the times one doesn't receive them, and for the instances when fine work of others doesn't get acknowledgment. But, that said, we were pretty happy about the Obies.

Well, anyway, it was a terrific experience.

SPECIFIC NOTES FOR ACTORS AND DIRECTORS

I am in the habit of writing notes to the acting editions of my plays in an attempt to offer what I would say to the director and actors of a future production if I were able to be present during their rehearsals. The notes are not meant to inhibit the creative impulses of either director or actor, but to help clarify any confusing aspects in the play or in its production, and to offer my ideas on what acting tone best serves my work. Words are only precise up to a point, so your common sense and aesthetic judgment will have to be your chief guide. But I hope you will read these notes as you might have a conversation with me at a preproduction meeting.

BETTE'S NAME.

I intend the name "Bette" to be pronounced as "Bet"—one syllable, which better contrasts with her nickname of Betsy.

Another pronunciation thing: please pronounce "Nikkos" as Nee-kos. Margaret may Americanize it as Nick-os, perhaps, but the others should get it right.

MUSIC.

Please use Richard Peaslee's music. (He is the distinguished composer of *Marat/Sade.*) The music box melodiousness of his "Bette and Boo" theme seems to set just the right tone for the play's opening; and yet the melody has an underlying poignance to it when it comes back later.

Jerry Zaks used a repeat of the theme played on piano (on tape) at the end of Act I, and again at the end of the play. The music helps the acts to end, and the theme's poignance is worth adding to those two moments as well. (I'm always upset when an audience doesn't know an act—or a play—is over; in this case, I know that the endings do play as endings with the proper directorial skill.)

Zaks started the music at the end of Act I somewhere around Bette saying, "Are you awake, Boo? Boo?"; and at the end of the play, right after Emily's "Let's say a prayer over her," and before Matt's final speech. I recommend the use of the music at the end of Act I, and request it at the end of Act II.

Zaks also used a recurring musical intro for the entrance of the characters into each of the hospital scenes (except the last one, Scene 32), which I also recommend. (It's actually a jaunty fragment of the "Bette and Boo" theme, and is in Peaslee's packet of music.)

THE OPENING.

The "Bette and Boo" theme at the opening of the play is sung through once, sweetly and simply, and then is sung again, more up-tempo, as a two-part round.

The opening moments are very nonrealistic. In Zaks's version, the wedding couple and the relatives and Father Donnally all stood close together on a group of steps in front of stained-glass windows, and sang looking straight out. (They were not specifically performing "for" the audience, they just sang straight out, that's all.)

When the characters call out to one another, it's as if they are all in isolation, calling out to their significant others, uncertain where the other is. They are not upset particularly, just desirous that they get a response—though Joan may be annoyed about Nikkos, and Emily may be somewhat worried as she usually is, and so on as is logical for the other characters. It will seem a little enigmatic to the audience, but it's meant to be so, and the enigmatic quality is a good setup for Matt's opening comments about looking for order.

In Zaks's version, Matt was able to be hidden behind the people on the steps, and make his first entrance coming from behind them (which was nice thematically, as Matt indeed has "come from" this group of people). If that didn't work in terms of your sightlines, just have Matt enter from offstage after the calling out, I would think.

THE SETTING.

I mentioned stained-glass windows above, so perhaps this is a good time to discuss the set.

Loren Sherman is a brilliant stage designer who, judging from his work on *Bette and Boo, Baby with the Bathwater,* and Peter Parnell's *Romance Language,* seems especially gifted in solving the problems presented by plays with many different settings that need to move quickly and fluidly.

In describing what he did, I do not mean to imply that his is the only solution or one you should try to copy, just that it should be of interest how his set addressed problems inherent in the script.

Sherman's set was a series of sliding maroon-colored panels that slid on a track recessed into a carpet that covered the stage. These panels were operated by stagehands who stood behind them, but it could be done mechanically as well.

The panels were used to change the stage space in numerous ways, to suggest all the various locales; importantly, they were designed and rehearsed so that the changes were just about instantaneous. With thirty-three scenes, eliminating "waits" between the scenes is of the highest importance.

There were three sets of panels: an upstage set, which created the back wall of the setting; a midstage set of panels; and a downstage set of panels.

The upstage, or back wall, panels were designed to be any of three things: first, a solid maroon background with three stained-glass windows, obviously suggesting a church; second, a solid background with one or more windows with venetian blinds and curtains on them, suggesting any of the home settings; and third, a solid maroon background with nothing on it, allowing for an "anyplace" setting.

The midstage and downstage sets of panels were also solid-colored with nothing on them, and were used to change and limit the stage space (and to allow stagehands to set up for the next scene behind them).

The "bigger" scenes were performed on the full playing space, using the upstage panels for the appropriate back wall, and with a few chosen furniture pieces. "Big" scenes included the wedding, Thanksgiving at Bette and Boo's house, the retreat, etc.—usually a scene with a lot of people or that "felt" big.

The "smaller" scenes took place in playing areas defined and limited by configurations of the panels.

In any case, these three rows of panels were used in an extremely complicated way to change the shape and size of the playing space in a split second. The logistics of how the furniture pieces were set up behind the closed panels so that when they opened the next set was already in place—these logistics are too complicated for me to articulate for the purposes of this essay.

However, I don't intend for you to copy this system, just to be aware how this panel system allowed for the stage space and setting to be changed instantaneously as far as the audience was concerned—which is my main concern. With thirty-three scenes, speed in going from scene to scene is of the essence.

In terms of other setting ideas, full realistic settings for any of the scenes would probably be wrong; there are just too many changes for "full" settings not to seem laborious. I'm pretty sure you want a "suggestive" setting for this play, one that changes its implications and looks easily.

One single setting (an all-purpose living room, perhaps) that with lighting and staging kept suggesting different locales would be fine with me, and a logical way to solve the problems in designing this play.

Or a totally nonrealistic space that had modulelike blocks that stood in for furniture (as is used in all plays at the O'Neill National Playwrights Conference, for instance), is also fine with me. I even suggested to Zaks and Sherman the rather crackpot notion of setting the play on a great big enormous wedding cake (with the characters able to sit or stand on the different "edges" of the cake); though that might be an extreme setting, it would have the benefit of standing in easily for all the different scene changes, without any waits for the audience, and that's my major concern. (I wouldn't want an all-purpose church setting, though, as that would overstate the Catholic influence in the play. With our use of the stained-glass windows, it was extremely important to me that they could also disappear when we wanted them to.)

One additional comment about Sherman's solution, though. Aside from the ability to keep the action moving with no stops, the sliding panels sometimes acted as punctuation to the end of a scene. (You could try to get a similar effect with lighting, or doors closing, I imagine.)

A BRIEF HARANGUE.

A stray note about the set. Please don't set the play "where Matt lives," wherever that may be. I saw a production of the full-length version that seemed to be in some depressing lower-class tenement, with a cheap kitchen table and a window center stage overlooking a brick wall and a fire escape. This was a "one-setting solution" (which I certainly don't object to), so all the scenes took place in this set. Aside from finding the set, though, extremely demoralizing to look at, I wondered why the director had decided that the Brennan and Hudlocke families were so poor; I thought of them as firmly in the middle class, even (especially the Hudlockes) upper-middle class.

I was flabbergasted when the director told me that the set didn't reflect the Brennans or Hudlockes at all but was "where Matt lived." Since there are no scenes where Matt lives, the audience (I am convinced) had no more idea than I did that this depressing abode represented Matt's apartment. So this bad idea was not even effectively communicated. But, more importantly, it is a very bad idea. Yes, the play in many ways *is* Matt's memory play, but to set the play "where Matt lives" makes as little sense as looking at Tom's last speech in *The Glass Menagerie* and then setting the whole play in Amsterdam.

This same production staged Scene 30 (Matt has dinner with Karl, Soot, Margaret, and Paul) with Karl and Margaret *not* at the table (though Soot and Paul were), and with Matt not at the table, but *lying on his back*, downstage, staring at the ceiling. His opening line, "Hello. Nice to see you all," was very confusing, as one didn't know to whom he was speaking. And since most of the time he didn't get to look at Karl (he finally got up off his back, after a while), the content of the scene never really took place.

The director explained this staging by saying he feared that the audience would think the scene "real" if Matt actually sat at the table; I pointed out to him that since there were two dead people at the table, it was not highly likely that the audience would think the scene "real."

Furthermore, his belief that he had to somehow specially address what was or wasn't "real," due to the fact that Matt is remembering some scenes and presumably imagining and/or exaggerating others—this belief was, I feel, an incorrect and dangerous side path he had wandered down. The director basically didn't trust the audience to make sense of this issue *as communicated by the script itself,* and felt he had to run around "interpreting" it for them with little signals. (The set and this scene were not the only examples. The last scene of the play, a rather realistic piece of writing, was staged Beckett-style, with all three characters sitting in chairs, staring straight ahead, never looking at one another. I don't know what that was supposed to do—perhaps remove the scene's natural warmth, which it certainly did.) What made it worse, he was talented, and he meant well. (I sound like Matt.) But it was not a happy meeting of play and director.

Some people, I'm told, bristle at the fact that I write these notes. As an actor, I can sympathize to some degree, and I don't want to straitjacket creativity. But seeing tenements "where Matt lives" and a dinner scene staged with none of the participants at dinner is an extremely painful experience for an author. If a director puts Hamlet on roller skates, or even if a director sets *Endgame* in a subway station—the plays are so famous one knows that it is a directorial interpretation, for good or bad. (And the subway setting, for instance, which Joanne Akalitis tried at American Repertory Theatre, even sounds interesting to me.) But if a director does a strange interpretation of a new play, the audience quite logically assumes that that is how the author wrote it. And I don't think that's fair.

And that's why I write these notes—probably not for the directors who would stage Matt lying on his back no matter what I said, but for people who might genuinely want to capture the tone I had in mind, and who don't mind some pointers in getting there.

Well, enough of that. But please don't set this play "where Matt lives," or in Matt's mind, or in Amsterdam. Please do not have people lie on their backs on the floor every time a direction says "at table." Thank you.

THE COSTUMES.

Thirty-three scenes spanning thirty years seems a nightmare in terms of changing costumes to keep up with the time span; plus, many of the scenes are so short, it's probably not even possible. Luckily, I don't think it's desirable either.

Costume designer William Ivey Long, in agreement with me and Zaks, chose to leave everyone in their wedding clothes, more or less, for the whole play. This was thematically appealing to me as well—we are always reminded of how the characters started out.

Though the characters' "core costumes" did indeed remain the same throughout, there were tiny changes for all that made for variety (and a rather significant change for Bette).

As the play went on, the removal of suit coats for the men, or of hats and veils and lace jackets for the women, made for a sense of variety, as well as let the characters look more relaxed for some scenes (when they're at home), and more formal for others (Soot and Margaret putting their hats back on for Thanksgiving, say, or for the early hospital scenes).

Further, there were certain small logical additions—Paul, usually a bit downtrodden, added to his costume a dumpy-looking cardigan sweater once he was rid of his wedding jacket. Likewise a loose, rather gloomy-looking sweater was eventually worn by the non-fashion-conscious Emily.

In designing the wedding clothes, Long made a conscious decision to give the characters good taste, with which I concur. I would be unhappy with cheap shots making fun of any corny clothing choices, or making any comments about vulgar 1950s garb (like those awful wide skirts that flair out on the sides, which make me think of 1955 movies). Indeed, since the wedding takes place in the late 1940s (judging from the chronology that Matt sputters out in Scene 31), Long pointed out to me that it would be a 1940s look that the wedding apparel would have, not a mid-50s Doris Day look.

The core costume used at the wedding should, though, not be distracting later in the play. For instance, if one dressed Emily and Joan in full-length bridesmaids' outfits, it would be problematic in the later scenes. So Long didn't give Emily and Joan floor-length gowns, but nonmatching (though pastel coordinated) normal-length dresses, with corsages and little lace jackets; the corsages and jackets were removed for later scenes.

Boo wore tails for the wedding itself, but by Scene 4, had removed his tailcoat to remain in just his vest and tie, then later removed the tie, then later, as his life disintegrated more, removed the vest and was just in his shirt sleeves. (He though, rather touchingly, dressed back up in his wedding garb for his final visit to Bette in the hospital.)

Bette's wedding dress was the larger problem. Long wanted a full-length full bridal gown look for Bette at the top of the play. I concurred, but felt that it would be too distracting in later scenes. (Imagine Bette striding around yelling, "You don't vacuum gravy" in a floor-length wedding gown. It *could* work, actually, I suppose, as a thematic statement, but the dangers for pretentiousness and ludicrousness are high.)

Long told me—as I didn't know—that particularly in the 1950s, women's magazines encouraged their readers to re-do their wedding gowns into cocktail dresses, so he decided to build Bette a dress that was normal length but otherwise copied her wedding dress. (For Act II, he gave her a light blue version of the same dress, as if she had dyed it somewhere along the way; Long added this just for variety.)

In dress rehearsals, I found the look of Bette's cocktail dress rather more formal-looking than I expected, and I felt that its relation to the wedding dress was not as obvious as I thought it would be. So on the night of the first preview, I asked Zaks and Long if I could add a line for Matt to say about Bette having refashioned her wedding gown at the suggestion of *Redbook*. I did this only for the sake of clarity, but discovered that the line played also as one of the biggest and most consistent laughs of the evening. Such are the joys of collaboration.

For the hospital scene at the end, Long designed a nightgown for Bette that was from the same cream-colored material as her wedding gown and had a similar neckline. Since Bette had been in light blue for all of Act II, the sudden return to wedding white coupled with Boo's return to his tails was very touching. (At the final dress, when Graham Beckel as Boo entered the hospital carrying a bouquet of flowers and dressed again in his tails, Joan Allen as Bette, seeing this costume choice for the first time, had to fight back tears in order to continue the scene.)

Another costume issue—the pregnancies of Joan and Bette. I think they should be noticeably pregnant when indicated in the script, but not overdone so as to be grotesque. (Whether Joan should look pregnant in the wedding scene I leave to your discretion. In Scene 6, Bette should not look pregnant yet; she has probably just learned she's expecting.)

For the Christmas at the Hudlockes' scene, the second pledge, and Joan's birthday party, it is important that Bette look pregnant. Unfortunately, Scene 23 ("Twenty years later, Bette has dinner with her son") comes in the middle of this, and Bette clearly must not look pregnant in the twenty years later scene. Our solution was to make a little pillow that fit under Bette's dress, attached around her waist with Velcro, and which was removable and replaceable quickly, offstage. If, for some reason, you had trouble with this, dispense with the pregnancy look for Christmas and the second pledge, and just use it for the birthday party, which is after Scene 23.

A final Bette costume issue. Karl must pour his drink on her at the end of Christmas. At the Public, her dress was Scotchgarded so that water literally ran off it, without damaging the dress. (She actually had two identical Act II dresses, one not Scotchgarded, so that she was not stuck in a wet dress if any of the water should fall onto the non-Scotchgarded part.)

The final costume issues are the doctor, the priest, and Matt.

The doctor is a small part, doubled by the actor who plays Father Donnally (for purposes of convenience, as well as a slight thematic tie of the doctor and priest being outside authorities who deal with Bette and Boo). The doctor's costume should be whatever says "doctor" quickly to the audience and makes it clear that it's not Father Donnally dressed differently.

Father Donnally is a parish priest, and as such has the normal black cassock that Bing Crosby wore in so many films (and so many priests wore in life, I suppose I should add). Zaks and I felt that the black cassock was a little drab for the opening, and so for that one he wore nice white-and-silver priest's wedding robes.

Matt is not dressed for the wedding, as he was not born at that point. Although if you wanted to dress him up out of "respect" for the event, that's okay. I rather prefer Long's solution, which was to dress him as "student," with clothes that clearly wouldn't fit in with the wedding picture.

Though Matt would have been in college in the 1960s, a full-out radical student look for him would not be a correct match with his personality. Long went for preppy casual—a nice sports jacket, a loosened tie over a blue workshirt, jeans. Long liked that the jeans in particular clashed visually with the wedding party, more than a dressier casual choice (khaki, corduroy) would have. Matt needn't—and shouldn't—change clothes for the duration of the play.

If you set the play in Amsterdam, Matt should wear a sailor suit and have tattoos saying MOTHER on his forearms. (Just kidding, just kidding!)

ANOTHER HARANGUE.

No, false alarm.

From here on in, I'm going to offer comments on miscellaneous issues, and will skip around rather.

THE HONEYMOON.

Zaks staged Scene 4 (the honeymoon, continued) with Bette and Boo in a bed, unlike how I had it in the script, which was Bette and Boo standing together wrapped in a sheet. I've left it the latter way in the script because I think it's easier to stage without a bed, but I have no objection to the scene taking place in a bed, if that works out for you.

However, either way (sheet or bed), I like the stylization of keeping Bette and Boo more or less still dressed in their wedding clothes. If you have them either in their underwear or, worse, with their shirts off, I find that that distracts from the content of the scene itself, and for the comedy in it as well. (It can turn it sniggering, which is unpleasant.) The scene certainly has a flirtatious feel to some of it, but it's really not *about* sex or "first time" at all. It's primarily about the workings of Bette's mind (charming but somewhat infantile).

THE HOSPITAL SCENES.

I envisioned the hospital "lineup" for every scene to be all the characters standing in a straight line, facing out to the audience, as if their backs were against a hospital hallway. This isn't a very realistic pose, but the stylization of it seems right for the scene, and the fact that we can always see their faces at the top of the scene waiting is also important. (I don't mean they stay frozen, staring out; they look at each other when they speak, and turn to the doctor when he comes out. I just mean they start out that way.)

The doctor, the script says, "drops the baby." He does not "throw" the baby down in anger, or disgust; or conversely, he does not toss it onto the ground with some fake cheeriness. He either shows no emotion or, maybe as time goes on, a little normal fatigue over doing the same thing over and over (but subtly). He announces the fact: "It's dead. The baby's dead." Then he lets go of the bundle that has been in his arms, and it drops to the floor. Let the action make the moment; don't color it in any particular way.

THE BABY PROP.

The original student production and Zaks's production did the baby prop as a believably shaped "bundle" that made a thud when dropped. It was constructed as a beanbag (I think), more or less in a baby's form, but *totally* wrapped in a blanket, so that one could not see any "baby" or beanbag. I'm sorry to be didactic, but I think that is the one way to design the baby.

If you use a real doll that you can see through an opening in the blanket (as I've seen), the first thing that happens is that the audience gasps because the image for a split second becomes too real—you think about the horror of dropping a real baby on the ground; then a second later, the audience reminds itself that the doll is, of course, fake and not a baby at all, and by then they're outside the play and not thinking about Bette or the dead baby or any of the characters onstage.

Using the visible doll made the audience react in two stages (within a few seconds), which is not good. When it is only the bundle that is dropped, the audience is able to react together at the same time on the same issue: they are shocked the baby is dead, they are shocked it has been dropped, they laugh that it has been dropped, they question whether it is appropriate to laugh that it has been dropped.

And using any very nonrealistic representation—like a basketball or something—is also not good: it will take us too far out of reality and be too jokey. For all the oddness of my representing the babies' deaths the way I have, it does still communicate that Bette has lost a child. A bouncing basketball would not do that well. (Plus, it should make a small thud sound when it hits—which will help trigger the audience's conflicted laughter; if it bounces, it's too farcical, too unreal.)

THE FAKE SCENE

Scene 22 (twenty years later, Bette also has dinner with his son) starts realistically enough, but starting with "You're right, it's not fair to bring up the children that died," it starts to shift to Matt's fantasy of a scene where his mother suddenly becomes super-reasonable and undemanding. Don't tip this to the audience too early. Let Bette play her first two long speeches as convincingly and as logically as possible. If she overdoes any of the comments, the audience will realize it's false too soon. I love instead the sort of cumulative doubt that creeps into the audience—you can feel them thinking, "This scene sounds a little false."

WHAT'S THE MATTER WITH YOU?

The end of Scene 23 when Bette and Boo's quarrel disintegrates into "What's the matter with you?", "What's the matter with you?", etc. When the actors convincingly are fighting, but just find themselves stuck making the same point back and forth, their genuine amusement seems a very good way to end the scene. Because it was hard to totally set that (faking the amusement seemed hard), Zaks and I let the actors keep adding "What's the matter with you?" (up to a reasonable point, three or four more than the script says) if that helps them. I also like it when Boo starts the laughter.

THE CHARACTERS:

MATT.

I'm pretty sure Matt should be onstage only when indicated in the script. If he's on for scenes where he's not written in—like his birth, for instance—it overdoes the "this is Matt's memory play" stuff.

It also fights against the unusual shape of the play. I think in Act I, it should feel like Bette's play; in Act II, it begins to feel like Bette *and* Matt's play; for a little while (from the divorce through the final baby), it starts to feel like Matt's play; and from Bette's entrance in Scene 32 on to the end, it feels like Bette and Matt's play again. (Boo is certainly terribly important, and part of the ending; but something more central seems to happen between Matt and Bette, I think.)

Matt starts the play believing he can make sense of things through analyzing them. As time goes on, this works less and less well for him, culminating in his "I can't make sense out of these things anymore" (a speech I wrote triggered by Joe Papp's comment that Matt should somehow "finish" with his Thomas Hardy stuff, a good comment).

Matt should have a sense of humor—if he seems only sensitive, I find the material becomes pleading and embarrassing (to me, at least). And much of the humor is in the deadpan delivery of comments, I believe.

And though I don't want Matt's position to become pathetic, still, from Thanksgiving on, there's no getting around that he suffers in the situations. Edith Oliver's description (in *The New Yorker)* of Matt watching—"sometimes visibly suffering, sometimes numb"—is appropriate, I think.

And the "sometimes numb" image is useful to keep in mind, to avoid any obvious pleading for sympathy; it's accurate as well—children in alcoholic homes often become quite stoic; everyone else around them is in such a mess, they don't want to be any bother, and so they become little adults. And speaking of little adults, it's also good to avoid actually *playing* Matt as a little boy; just keep it simple for the "arts and crafts" scene, and by the time we're to Thanksgiving he's already the little adult.

Zaks encouraged me and Joan Allen as Bette not to shrink away from rather full-anger choices in the Bette-Matt arguments (especially in Scenes 22, 32, and the brief disagreement about healing and prayer in 33).

I resisted this direction at first, due to fear that full out anger might seem too "Oh pity poor Matt"; in playing it, I decided Zaks was very right, and that the full anger made the play not sentimental, just honest. (Damn it, though, it's so tricky passing this sort of advice on. I saw two Matts who did "My favorite movie is *Citizen Kane*, I don't call you 'Citizen Kane'" with genuine anger, and the line still got the appropriate laugh I think it should get; I saw another Matt do the same line with similar anger, and yet due to some overseriousness that the actor communicated, the line was not at all funny, and, alas, I think that's wrong. And I can't prove that to you, or tell you exactly how to do it right.)

One last thing about Matt. His final speech ("Bette passed into death and is with God") has *no* irony in it. The impulse behind it is to share with the audience the only comfort human beings have found to cope with death—the belief in an afterlife. Matt has made clear that he doesn't seem to believe in all that, *but that fact doesn't belong in this moment*. The moment is about sharing with the audience the sense of loss; perhaps for the moment, Matt decides to believe in heaven—or to speak as if he believes because it's the only comfort available, the only thing he can think to say. Any sense of "Matt looks down or separates himself from those who believe" (which appeared in guess which favorite production) is totally at odds with what I mean by the moment.

BETTE.

Before starting to cast Bette, Zaks and I agreed we were looking for someone who seemed like a "winner." (And Joan Allen, a fabulous actress, is very much a winner.) Part of Bette's story is that she is someone for whom things basically should have and could have gone right. She is thus genuinely charming, very vivacious, etc.; it just all goes very wrong. But, for all her chatter, she is not stupid. She comes from a background where the chatter is considered part of a woman's charm, and where no one is expected to have to make thoughtful decisions as nothing problematic is supposed to happen.

If she's not stupid, though, she is also not wise. Karl is partially right in Scene 30—she keeps trying for far too long to change things she can't change (Boo's drinking, having another child against medical likelihood). But unlike the other characters, she is in there trying, and that's something.

We should, of course, feel for her. She can act like a bitch often, but that's not, at core, what she is. Joan Allen can yell with the best of them when the script calls for that, but she also had an extraordinary vulnerability somewhere within Bette's iron will that made Bette's plight extremely moving.

BOO.

Boo is at core very sweet, and he probably loves Bette very much (Graham Beckel was terrific looking at Bette with infatuation in the honeymoon scene). However, his personality never confronts anything—he seems totally inured to watching his father insult his mother, for instance (though, of course, he would have had many years getting used to it).

He drinks, presumably, to escape, and Bette keeps on and on at him trying to keep him from escaping; and in that way, they are deeply incompatible.

I was grateful that Beckel as an actor never made a fuss about how passive Boo is, particularly in the Hudlocke scenes; he took it as a given of Boo's character, which I think it is. His mother laughs when awful things are said; Boo either doesn't listen, or takes a drink.

Beckel also was very painful to watch in the divorce scene and in the final baby scene; his Boo, when circumstances *forced* him to see something irrevocable, had hurt eyes.

Zaks made a terrific point about the last scene. For all the fact that Boo keeps staring off suddenly, most of the time he and Bette have a lovely ease between them in this final scene that, in Zaks's words, made you wish that they had found a way to get that ease earlier. His seeing that ease was important for this scene—because for all the sadness in the situation, the sadness isn't what to play (except for the occasional inescapable moments). Bette has given up trying to change Boo, and that has allowed her to enjoy his affection for the first time in ages. It's a scene that shows that a reconciliation among all three has sort of happened—not a triumphant one, because everyone has lowered their stakes and expectations, but a reconciliation nonetheless.

SOME OF THE OTHER CHARACTERS.

SOOT. Soot's laugh is terribly important, and an integral part of her character. Don't cast an actress who can't or won't do the laugh. Also, please have Soot do the "Oh, Karl" (laughs) lines as written—that is, she says "Oh, Karl," and *then* laughs; the laugh and the line should be separated.

Soot is one of my favorite characters (and usually one of the audience's as well).

Many of us would gather offstage nightly to watch certain of Olympia Dukakis's scenes, she was so remarkable. I was particularly enamored of how she would look over at Karl every time he began to speak with this expression of pleased expectation, as if she knew that whatever was about to come out of his mouth was, without question, certain to be the most delightful and charming remark imaginable. She would then listen with rapt attention as he said his usually horrible or insulting comment, and then she would laugh delightedly *as if* her pleased expectation had been totally correct. Occasionally, if her line was a slight reproach of Karl—such as "You shouldn't tease everyone so"—her attitude seemed to be that Karl had just said something slightly naughty but still vastly amusing, while what any sane person would have heard was that Karl had just been shocking and cruel.

This extremely crazy disparity between what Karl says and how she responds is the core of Soot's character. It's hilarious and, without the actress having to push it, sort of heartbreaking.

KARL. A major thing about Karl—cast him as intelligent and upper-class. (Soot should be upper-class as well.) He is *not* meant to be a lower-class Archie Bunker, uncouth and stupid. He is mean to his wife and to others because he is a misanthrope; I think he looked at the world early in life, didn't like what he saw, and out of that perception began to watch everything around him like a scientist looking at bugs through a microscope. But he *is* smart.

Along these lines, I recall Bill Moor listening to Bette rattle on about having more children and about Jackie Cooper's cuteness versus Shirley Temple's (Scene 14), and seeing on his face, subtly, the thought that Bette was very stupid for making these decisions about having children. You saw the opinion on his face—and this opinion was a more genuine response to what was going on in the room than anything that was coming from anyone else in the scene: Boo is drinking and trying not to listen, and Soot, who can't stand any problems of any sort, is smiling at Bette as if everything she was saying was delightful. Of course, Karl follows this silent reaction by being very insulting to Bette, which doesn't particularly help anyone; but the insult comes from a genuine opinion about how foolishly she is running her life.

Another choice Bill Moor made that was useful, I think, was that he decided that Karl was, most times, amused by Soot. This helped explain what kept them together, probably. Karl is a realist and sees things, he just doesn't believe anything can be done about anything, and so he has chosen to be nasty. Soot can't stand reality because most things frighten her, and so she pretends to herself (so successfully that she doesn't even know she's pretending) that everything is fine with everything. In a strange way, they certainly "go" together.

The characters of the Brennan family and Father Donnally are seemingly less open to misunderstanding, and so I'll spend less time on them.

PAUL is a kind father, and most of the lines I've given him are actually rather sensible, it's just nobody can understand him. Bill McCutcheon seemed sweet and fond of his girls. He also always looked very irritated whenever Margaret told him not to speak, and would mutter to himself, which was a funny choice.

A stray thing about Paul's speech. I describe how I envision it in the script, in terms of Paul's dropping most of his consonants so that it is mostly impossible to understand him. I have seen some actors do that but then add to it a staccato, jerky rhythm to how Paul speaks. I would prefer your Paul not do this—it sounds slightly retarded to me, which is wrong (Paul's mind is absolutely fine), or else like an actor's choice that I just don't "get." Plus, the staccato rhythms very much hurt the divorce scene where Paul's rhythms should be very much like an old-time lawyer—conversational, making points, talking to the judge, etc.; it's just he's incomprehensible. (McCutcheon was hilarious as this frustrated lawyer; if we all watched Olympia's scenes, I noted that she always stood offstage to watch that scene.)

So, if you would, I prefer normal speaking rhythms (just lose most of the consonants.)

JOAN is a smallish part, and, judging by auditions, a little hard to get a handle on. However, the actresses we called back all had in common an extremely dry delivery and the ability to make the force of Joan's unhappiness and edgy bitterness *funny*. Probably Joan liked somebody in the world once, but it's not shown in this play. Mercedes Ruehl gave an indelible performance, and it's a tribute to her gifts how much she was noticed in this part. Also, early laughs in a play are important to cue the audience "what kind of play this is going to be," and Joan's character (and Margaret's) have a lot of lines that are laugh lines *depending* on how you say them. ("She does. You look lovely, Bette" is funny when said with the proper, flat, semi-hostile disinterest. Oh God, he's giving line readings now.)

MARGARET says, "Let's not talk about it" many times in the play, whenever anyone brings up a problem. Soot pretends (or has convinced herself) the problems aren't there. Margaret does see them, it's just that she is of the old school who feels you shouldn't talk about unpleasant things. Patricia Falkenhain was hilariously on the nose when, for instance, in Thanksgiving she'd tell Bette that she and Skippy might stay with her to

avoid Boo's drunkenness, and then a moment later says with
utter cheeriness as if nothing has happened, "Good-bye, Boo!"

As Margaret lets drop in her longest speech (Scene 24), she
likes her children to have problems, it makes her feel needed.
That speech is one of the meannest I've ever written, I think,
but it *does* happen that way; and Patricia Falkenhain's charm
was the absolute appropriate interpretation of it—Margaret *is*
charming, she *is* a caring mother, she just wants to be the
queen bee, so she likes all the bickering that goes on around
her.

EMILY. Audiences love Emily. She is dear, and doesn't seem
to have a mean bone in her body. But her mind sure is mucked-
up, and writing her I was reminded of a comment a friend
once made about a poignant character in a movie (Shirley
Knight in *Petulia*, mistreated by her husband George C. Scott):
I was saying how touching I found her vulnerability, and my
friend (a woman) said, yes, she supposed so but one also felt the
satisfaction of seeing a sensitive person "get it." I thought this
remark was rather shocking, but also rather true.

Emily obviously works out of guilt, very misplaced and
deeply rooted. She's also rather childlike—her mind seems to
move slower than other people's, and she has a child's belief
that everything is connected to her (and, in her case, is her
fault). I adored watching Kathryn Grody as Emily trying desperately to make sense of what Father Donnally was saying,
and always presuming that if she didn't follow it, it must be her
fault (ergo, all her hand raisings).

Zaks and Kathryn also made Emily strong in the last scene;
she knows about prayer, and about offering comfort, and so
there was no apologetic quality to any of her behavior in the
last scene; she was (in a nice way) in her element.

FATHER DONNALLY was Richard B. Shull. Shull is like one
of the marvelous character actors in films from the 1930s and
40s; though his priest was often kindly to Bette (and others),
irritation is always not too far below the surface; the last third
of Shull's marriage retreat was a hilarious explosion of built-up
irritation at his intolerable position, being asked to solve impossible problems. If he joined Karl at dinner in Scene 30, they
would have had some points of agreement about not being
able to change some things (although Donnally is basically
kindly).

AND NOW THE END.

I really must apologize. I have gone on too long, and though I've tried to edit this (and have cut some stuff, believe it or not), I have fussed and fussed with this for too long, and so I've decided to leave it lengthy so you can choose what to make use of, and what to reject.

I really do know that there is rarely only one way to do something in acting and directing—but within that range of possibilities, there really are, I think, choices that hit the right tone for my stuff, and choices that make it fall flat, or go nasty or go silly. That's what I'm trying to control. Children of alcoholics, I have read, often have trouble in later life trying to overcontrol things, and I guess this essay is a bit of an example of that. But at least I'm not coming to your house directly, to bother you; and at least I got to praise the actors who worked with such commitment on the play at the Public, and to whom I offer much affection and gratitude.

Christopher Durang
November 1985